Gregory Palamas

The Triads

EDITED WITH AN INTRODUCTION BY
JOHN MEYENDORFF

TRANSLATION BY
NICHOLAS GENDLE

PREFACE BY
JAROSLAV PELIKAN

PAULIST PRESS
NEW YORK • RAMSEY • TORONTO

203377

Library of Congress
Catalog Card Number 82-61741

ISBN: 0-8091-2447-5 (paper)
        0-8091-0328-1 (cloth)

Published by Paulist Press
545 Island Road, Ramsey, N.J. 07446

Printed and bound in the
United States of America

Contents

The Translator of this Volume
NICHOLAS GENDLE is engaged in teaching and research in Patristics and Byzantine studies at Oxford University, where he has been teaching Byzantine art since 1974. After completing his doctoral studies at Oxford, he received research fellowships at Edinburgh University and the Catholic University of America. His thesis, *The Apophatic Approach to God in the Greek Fathers*, is currently appearing in consecutive numbers of the journal *Church and Theology;* he has also published *Icons in Oxford* (1980) and articles on the Byzantine Saints, the role of art in the early church and patristic psychology. He is presently working to complete a book on Byzantine image theory, begun at the Dumbarton Oaks Center, Washington D.C.

Editor and Author of the Introduction
JOHN MEYENDORFF is Professor of History, Fordham University and Professor of Patristics and Church History, St. Vladimir's Seminary, Tuckahoe, New York. He received the degree of *Docteur ès-lettres* at the Sorbonne, Paris in 1958 and has been on the faculty of Harvard University, Center for Byzantine Studies, Dumbarton Oaks (1960–67) where he also served as acting Director of Studies (1978). Father Meyendorff is an internationally esteemed authority on Eastern Christian History, Theology and Spirituality and a corresponding Fellow, The British Academy. His books include *St. Gregory Palamas and Orthodox Spirituality* (1959), *Gregory Palamas* (1959), *The Orthodox Church* (1963), *Orthodoxy and Catholicity* (1966), *Christ in Eastern Christian Thought* (1969), *Byzantine Theology* (1974), *Byzantine Hesychasm* (1974), and *Byzantium and the Rise of Russia* (1981).

Author of the Preface
JAROSLAV PELIKAN received his Ph.D. in 1946 from the University of Chicago, where he also taught from 1953 to 1962. Since 1962 he has been a member of the faculty of Yale University, where he is now Sterling Professor of History. He was Editor of the American edition of *Luther's Works*, and is a member of the editorial board for *The Collected Works of Erasmus*. Of his books, the best known is probably *The Christian Tradition: A History of the Development of Doctrine* (1971ff.), projected for five volumes. In addition to the second volume of that set, *The Spirit of Eastern Christendom (600–1700)*, his publications in the history of Christian doctrine in the East include a monograph on Athanasius, an edition of Chrysostom's commentary on the Sermon on the Mount, and numerous essays dealing with thinkers from Gregory of Nyssa and Basil of Caesarea through Maximus Confessor to Dostoevsky and Tolstoy. He is also serving as editor for the volume *Maximus Confessor* in the present series.

Foreword

The aim of this volume is to produce an anthology of the positive teaching of St. Gregory Palamas for the modern educated reader. The texts, which have been chosen by John Meyendorff, are all taken from Palamas's *Triads in Defence of the Holy Hesychasts,* and translated from Meyendorff's critical edition (Grégoire Palamas, *Défense des saints hésychastes,* 2nd ed., Spicilegium Sacrum Lovaniense, études et documents, fascicules 30 and 31, Louvain 1973).

In rendering this material into English, I have tried to stay as close as possible to the Greek text, while bearing in mind that one is translating ideas and not words. I have taken the liberty of occasionally eliminating passages that are of a purely rhetorical and polemical nature, and such omissions are indicated in our text by ellipsis points. At the same time, I am aware that we are dealing here with an apologetic tract, and it would not be right to remove all references to the views of Palamas's protagonist, the monk Barlaam, and to the historical debate with him that gave rise to the *Triads.* Similarly, while it has sometimes been necessary to split up some of the original long sentences into shorter English sentences, an attempt has been made to retain something of the literary flavour of the Greek. This style will admittedly sound strange to modern ears at times, as will the language of some of the earlier Fathers cited by Palamas, especially perhaps St. Dionysius (or Denys) the Areopagite.

With problems of comprehension by those not familiar with patristic literature in mind, I have tried to provide something of a commentary on the text in the footnotes, elucidating key ideas and attempting to clarify some of the more difficult passages. I am well

FOREWORD

aware that much more could have been done in the way of comment, had space allowed. At any rate, the opportunity to write *some* footnotes has enabled me to avoid cumbersome periphrases in translating technical phrases that occur with some frequency. The biblical and patristic references in the notes are mostly derived from Fr. Meyendorff's edition, cited above.

I should like to take this opportunity to thank Archimandrite Kallistos Ware of Oxford University, who has read the whole work in typescript and made numerous useful suggestions. Such understanding of Palamas as I possess derives very largely from my long discussions with him about the meaning of the text; and also from my sessions on Byzantine theology with Fr. Meyendorff during 1978, a very happy year spent at Dumbarton Oaks, the Harvard Byzantine Institute. Needless to say, I accept entire responsibility for such errors as remain in the translation and notes. I should also like to express my gratitude to Miss Sally Purcell, an ideal academic typist, who has coped with my problematic manuscript with patience and skill.

If this book succeeds in making the thought of the last great Byzantine theologian better known and understood by modern English-speaking readers, then the effort spent on preparing it will have been amply repaid. For the translator at least, the business of coming to grips with the often difficult text of Palamas has led to the conviction that here we are dealing, not merely with an interesting chapter in the history of ideas, but with a permanent spiritual treasure of the Universal Church.

Preface

The rehabilitation of Gregory Palamas in the Western Church during the twentieth century is a remarkable event in the history of scholarship, and the inclusion of a volume of Palamas in a series bearing the title "Classics of Western Spirituality" is itself a remarkable symbol of that rehabilitation.

During most of the six hundred years since the death of Gregory Palamas, the standard interpretation of his spirituality and theology among Western theologians and scholars has been colored by the polemics of his adversary, Barlaam.[1] Even those scholars, such as Martin Jugie,[2] who took the time to read in Palamas were bemused by the doctrine of "uncreated light" and more generally by the notion of "divine energies," seeing in such formulations a dangerous impairment of the Nicene doctrine of God. The article "Hesychasm" in *The Catholic Encyclopedia*, written by a thoughtful student of the Christian East, the distinguished liturgical scholar Adrian Fortescue (1874–1923), may serve as an example of how this history was interpreted to the general reader. The Synod of Constantinople in 1368, according to Fortescue, "canonized Palamas as a Father and Doctor of the Church." Fortescue continues: "So by the end of the fourteenth century Hesychasm had become a dogma of the Orthodox Church. It is so still. The interest in the question gradually died out, but . . . the real distinction between God's essence and operation remains one more principle, though it is rarely insisted on now, in which the Orthodox differ from Catholics. Gregory Palamas is a saint to them."[3]

But now, apparently, he is becoming a saint to increasing parts of the Western Church as well—an uncanonized saint, to be sure, but one who deserves attention as something more than a museum piece from Mount Athos. The successor to *The Catholic Encyclopedia* as a standard work of general reference, the *New Catholic Encyclopedia*, comments, in an article by the Dominican scholar Daniel Honorius Hunter: "Palamite doctrine on the divine nature of the light of Mt. Tabor and the visible presence of uncreated grace in the pure of heart has been an obstacle for Western theologians in accepting Palamas as a teacher of orthodoxy. On the other hand, Palamas's insistence that the whole man is engraced, body and soul, and the stress that he placed on the role of the body in prayer has been adopted in the West by recent theologians."[4] It is instructive to contemplate some of the possible reasons for this change of attitude during the half-century or so between the two encyclopedias.

The Second Vatican Council must certainly rank high among such reasons. Some future Ph.D. dissertation will have to deal with a comparison between the documentation for the decrees of the First Vatican Council and the documentation for those of the Second. The sheer statistical differences would, I am sure, be impressive: a quantum leap in the number of citations from Scripture; a similar improvement in the quantity (not even to mention the quality) of references to the liturgy as the *lex orandi* confirming the *lex credendi;* and a noteworthy expansion of the list of Eastern Church Fathers who belong to the Catholic tradition. Despite the unfortunate perpetuation, in the very first sentence of the decree on the East, of the paternalistic-sounding distinction between "Catholic [=Latin]" and "Oriental [=non-Latin],"[5] there is an explicit acknowledgement of "the ecclesiastical and spiritual patrimony" of the Eastern Churches, which applies, presumably, also to those parts of the Eastern "patrimony" that have not made as large a contribution to Western spirituality as they should have made.[6] And among these, Hesychasm must hold a notable position, not least because of the misunderstanding and even misinterpretation to which it has been subjected.

Yet the Council is both an expression and a source of other changes in the atmosphere. The striking description of Palamite thought as "a personal existentialism, applying the concept of divine 'simplicity' not to the essence but to the personal Divine Being which is revealed both in essence and in free acts—or energies—of God ... [and] thinking of God Himself in existential terms, while holding to His absolute transcendence,"[7] suggests another source: the recognition among all Christian groups of the neglected "existential" dimen-

PREFACE

sion in Christian thought. That recognition has come by various channels. For many in my generation, it was Søren Kierkegaard who first awakened this awareness; for me personally, because of my family roots, Fyodor Dostoevsky, whom I studied before ever hearing of Kierkegaard, performed this service; and, through the thought of men like Gabriel Marcel, many Roman Catholic thinkers—even those with a Thomistic and supposedly "essentialist" orientation, like Etienne Gilson and, in his own special way, Jacques Maritain—were arguing "that a Christian's philosophy is 'existential' in its own right."[8] In such an atmosphere, the voice of Gregory Palamas could come through with a new clarity and force.

It was able to come through, however, only because it was meanwhile being studied and interpreted with a new zeal, as attested by the footnotes in the present volume citing the works of Western scholars, above all perhaps Irénée Hausherr.[9] But the revival of Palamas was in part also related to another movement of the period between World War I and World War II, the emigration of Russian theologians and scholars to the West after the Russian Revolution.[10] If the Russian "*émigré* literature of the 1920's and 1930's appears in retrospect as an unbelievable and heroic phenomenon,"[11] the *émigré* scholarship of Russian theologians, above all in Paris, performed a similarly "heroic" task in making available the riches of Eastern spirituality and theology.[12] For the understanding of Gregory Palamas, it was the work of Vladimir Lossky (1903–1958) that made one of the most important early contributions. His essay of 1945, now available in English under the title "The Theology of Light in the Thought of St. Gregory Palamas,"[13] brought the analytic power of a fine philosophical and theological mind to bear on the explanation of Palamite teachings to Western scholars. But (if it will not transgress the bounds of scholarly propriety or strain the ties of friendship) I am obliged to say that the most substantial contribution to the historical and theological appreciation of Gregory Palamas in the West has been the scholarship, on both sides of the Atlantic, of John Meyendorff.

I am pleased and honored to salute this volume as the most recent fruit of that scholarship.

Introduction

A major spiritual and intellectual figure of Orthodox Byzantium, Gregory Palamas—monk, archbishop and eminent theologian—dedicated most of his active life to theological argument, centered on one basic truth: The living God is accessible to personal experience, because He shared His own life with humanity.

Both his contemporaries and the later generations considered that the nine treatises composed by Palamas between 1338 and 1341 and entitled *For the Defence of Those Who Practice Sacred Quietude* (*Hyper tōn hierōs hesychazontōn*) are the most important of all his writings. Since they were published in three groups of three books to rebuke first the oral teaching, then the written polemics of the Calabrian philosopher Barlaam, they are frequently referred to as the *Triads*. The Greek term *hesychia* ("quietude") is found in monastic literature since the fourth century to designate the mode of life chosen by hermits, dedicated to contemplation and constant prayer. Such monks were also known for centuries as *hesychasts*. Barlaam had denied the legitimacy of their spiritual methods and their claims to experience divine presence. Palamas stood up to defend them.

The extensive excerpts from the *Triads* translated and published in this book introduce the reader into the very substance of religious experience of the Christian East.

The hesychast tradition

Solitary life in the Egyptian or the Palestinian deserts was the original form of Christian monasticism. Already in the fourth centu-

1

ry, it was adopted by St. Anthony, who according to his biographer, St. Athanasius the Great, was the founder of the monastic movement, and became the model of all later anchorites. The appearance of the cenobitic monasticism with St. Pachomius, who in Egypt founded the first disciplined communities of monks, did not prevent further development of eremitism and the coexistence, throughout the Christian East, of both cenobites and anchorites throughout the early Christian centuries and the Middle Ages.

The term *hesychast* (*hesychastēs*) was used to designate a "hermit" or an anchorite from the very beginnings of monastic history. Together with *hesychia* it appears in the writings of Evagrius[1] (fourth c.), of St. Gregory of Nyssa[2] and in imperial legislation referring to monastic status.[3]

Among all the early teachers of monastic spirituality, Evagrius Ponticus formulated, better than any other, that fundamental doctrine on prayer which would inspire the hesychasts in all later centuries. According to Evagrius, prayer is "the highest act of the mind", the activity "appropriate to the dignity of the mind", an "ascent of the mind to God". "The state of prayer", he wrote, "can be aptly described as a habitual state of imperturbable calm. It matches to the heights of intelligible reality the mind which loves wisdom and which is truly spiritualized by the most intense love."[4]

According to Evagrius, a permanent "prayer of the mind", or "mental" prayer (*noera proseuchē*), is the goal, the content and the justification of hesychastic, eremitic life. He sees it as "natural" to the human mind. In prayer, man becomes truly himself by reestablishing the right and natural relationship with God.[5]

Modern historical scholarship has shown that the doctrine on prayer found in Evagrius, was, in fact, an expression of peculiar Origenistic metaphysics, based on Neoplatonism, which conceived the "mind" as naturally divine and as having originally existed without matter, so that the present material world is nothing but a consequence of the Fall.[6] Actually, Evagrius was even formally condemned by the ecumenical council of 553 because of his Origenism. Nevertheless, his writings on prayer remained extremely popular, and were often circulating under pseudonyms, particularly that of St. Neilos of Sinai. This does not mean, however, that their readers shared the author's metaphysical presuppositions. In the mainstream of the Eastern spiritual tradition, the mental prayer of Evagrius began to be understood and practiced in the context of a Christocentric spirituality. The "mind" ceased to be opposed to matter, because Christian monasticism fully accepted the implications of the Incarnation. Thus, the "mental prayer", addressed by Evagrius to the Deity, which he understood in a Neoplatonic and spiritualized sense, became the "prayer of *Jesus*".

In the late fourth century, this evolution of hesychast spirituality in the direction of Christocentrism was greatly influenced by the writings of an unknown author who used the pseudonym St. Macarius the Great. The writings of Ps. Macarius, very often quoted by Palamas, are rather different from the Neoplatonic intellectualism of Evagrius: The center of human consciousness and of divine presence in man is seen as occurring not in the "mind", but in the "heart". On this point, Macarius uses a vocabulary closer to the language of the Psalms (and of Jewish anthropology in general) than of Neoplatonism.[7] In Christianity, one tastes the grace of God, he writes, and sees that the Lord is sweet (Ps. 34:9). This tasting is the dynamic power of the Spirit manifesting itself in full certitude in the heart. The sons of light, ministers of the New Covenant in the Holy Spirit, have nothing to learn from men; they are "taught by God" (Isa. 54:13, Jn. 6:45). Grace itself engraves the laws of the Spirit on their hearts. . . . In fact, "the heart is master and King of the whole bodily organism, and when grace takes possession of the pasture-land of the heart, it rules over all its members and all its thoughts; for it is in the heart that the mind dwells, and there dwell all the soul's thoughts; it finds all its goods in the heart. That is why grace penetrates all the members of the body."[8]

In Macarius, the goal of prayer is not the disincarnation of the mind, but a transfiguration of the entire person—soul and body—through the presence of the incarnated God, accessible to the conscious "certitude of the heart".

Side by side with great monastic personalities, and communities that remained firmly in the framework of orthodox Christianity, early Christian monasticism also witnessed the appearance of sectarian groups. Some forces of monastic spirituality consciously opposed personal religious experience to the sacramental and hierarchical structure of the Church. Of particular significance, in this respect, was the so-called Messalian movement, which denied the necessity of baptism and other sacraments, rejected the need for social responsibility and recognized only charismatic leadership, as distinct from the teachings and pastoral ministry of bishops and priests. Throughout the Middle

Ages, the Messalians, also known as "Euchites" or "Bogomils" (or "Cathars" in the West), also promoted dualistic conceptions, rooted in Manicheism.

The attempts of some modern scholars to interpret the writings of Ps. Macarius himself as a Messalian document seem unconvincing to this author.[9] It remains, however, that the problem of a possible connection between Messalianism and some branches of hesychasm is not new. In particular, Barlaam the Calabrian himself accused the Byzantine hesychasts, his contemporaries, of being Messalians. It seems, in fact, that he envisaged any claim of real and conscious experience of God as a form of Messalianism. Palamas had no difficulty in showing that Orthodox hesychasts shared neither the antisacramentalism of the Messalians, nor their particular pretention to see the very essence of God with their material eyes. He did not deny, however, that on the popular level some contacts between the Messalians and the orthodox monastic milieus were very possible: We will see below that he may have been personally involved in such contacts himself.

In any case, the historical significance and influence of the writings of Ps. Macarius was not in promoting heretical Messalianism, but in reorienting the mystical tradition of the Evagrian type toward a more Christocentric and sacramental understanding of prayer. Thus, the great teachers of the Jesus Prayer, or "prayer of the heart", in the following centuries were men like St. Diadochus of Photice (fifth c.) and St. John Climacus (580–650), who generally maintained the hesychast tradition in the biblical and incarnational context, proper to the Greek patristic thought.[10] It was basically a simple though difficult discipline of "keeping one's mind in the heart", of "placing" there the Name of Jesus—since the Name of God is identified with the presence of the Divine Person itself—or of "attaching the Name of Jesus to one's breath" (St. John Climacus). The Jesus prayers also took the form of a constant mental repetition of a brief sentence such as "Lord Jesus Christ, Son of God, have mercy on me, a sinner."

The spirituality centered on the Jesus Prayer, which originated in eremitic monasticism and became a constant practice not only in cenobitic monasteries but also among the laity. Its simplicity and directness pointed at the essential content of the Christian faith and led to that personal experience of God without which—according to St. Symeon the New Theologian (949–1022)—there is no true Christianity.

INTRODUCTION

In the late thirteenth century, some written "methods" of the Jesus Prayer also propose a breathing technique aimed at attaching prayer to a constant physiological element of human life: the act of inhaling air. The exact meaning of this technique, which has been compared to *yoga*, was often misunderstood—perhaps by some of its unsophisticated practitioners, and in any case by Barlaam, who attacked it violently. This explains one of the major themes of the *Triads* of Palamas, which aimed at defining the role of the human body in prayer and, consequently, in a Christocentric conception of human life in its wholeness.

The life of Palamas

Born in 1296, in Constantinople, in a noble family close to the court of Emperor Andronicus II, Gregory lost his father at the age of seven, but continued his education at imperial expense.[11] The usual Byzantine curriculum included a thorough study of the *Logics* of Aristotle, and the young Gregory excelled in it. At the age of twenty, however, he decided to adopt the monastic life and persuaded all the other living members of his family—mother, two brothers and two sisters—to follow his example.

On Mount Athos, he joined the community of the oldest and remotest of all Athonite monasteries, the "Great Lavra" of St. Athanasius. He also spent some time as a hermit at the *skete* of Glossia, also on Mount Athos. Around 1325, Turkish raids on the Athonite peninsula obliged many monks to leave the Holy Mountain. Gregory and some friends found refuge in Thessalonica, where they formed a spiritual circle, based on prayer, and established connections in the city. Writers hostile to Palamas associate some of his activities during that period with "Bogomil", or "Messalian", sectarians mentioned earlier. It will be shown later that Palamas very clearly rejected the doctrinal views of the sectarians.

Palamas's own Orthodox commitment is further demonstrated by the fact of his ordination to the priesthood, at the canonical age of thirty (1326). Together with a few other monks, he then lived in a hermitage near Berrhea, following the pattern of "hesychast" life inherited from earlier centuries. Each week, for five days, he practiced the ideally uninterrupted "prayer of Jesus" in his hermitage, rejoining his community on Saturday and Sunday for Eucharistic and human fellowship with the brethren. By 1331, Gregory returned to Mount

INTRODUCTION

Athos, where he followed the same mode of life at the hermitage of St. Sabbas near his original monastery, the Lavra. Having acquired some prestige within the Athonite community, Gregory began to publish writings of hagiography and spirituality. He became for a brief period (1335–1336) abbot of the monastery of Esphigmenou. Soon, however, he was drawn into the arena of theological controversy, ecclesiastical strife and political turmoil, which would dominate the rest of his life, without changing anything of his spiritual commitments and theological persuasion.

The debate between Palamas and the Greek Italian "philosopher", Barlaam the Calabrian, began as a debate on theological method. Both men were engaged in discussing the problem of the Latin addition of the *Filioque*—"the Holy Spirit who proceeds from the Father *and the Son*"—to the original text of the Creed. However, for Barlaam—who, as Palamas, defended the Greek view—the issue was one of dialectic proof on the basis of scriptural or patristic statements, since no direct knowledge of God, of the relations between the persons of the divine Trinity, was accessible to the human mind. Palamas, on the contrary, approached theology not only as a conceptual exercise based on "revealed premises," but also, and primarily, as an expression of true Christian experience. Using the same technical Aristotelian terms as his opponent, Palamas insisted that theological discourse concerning the Trinity could reach *apodictic* (and not only *dialectic*) conclusions, that is, it could lead to *Truth itself.* The character of this discussion has led some historians to establish a parallel with the controversies between Nominalists and Realists in the contemporary Latin West, even though the context and character of the two debates are clearly different.

Barlaam resented the challenge presented to him by monks, whom he saw as intellectually unqualified fanatics. When he attempted to learn more about the hesychast methods of prayer—the basis of the "experience" to which they were always referring—he was shocked even more profoundly, particularly by the claim that the human body, and not only the mind, could be transfigured by divine light and contribute to the knowledge of God. It is this discussion that led not only to the writings of the *Triads* by Palamas, but also to the involvement of both Church and society in the debate.

In June and July 1341, two successive councils, held in Constantinople, rebuked Barlaam, who left Byzantium and ended his days

INTRODUCTION

in Italy. However, as his defense of the hesychasts seemed to have triumphed, Palamas became deeply entangled in the consequences of a civil war, which followed the sudden death of Emperor Andronicus III (1341). The most important political personality of the court, the Grand Domesticus John Cantacuzenos—a supporter of intellectuals who originally patronized Barlaam, but eventually sided with the monks—was dismissed by a Regency that included patriarch John Calecas. Palamas, seen as a friend and supporter of Cantacuzenos, was condemned and imprisoned, whereas the patriarch gave support to his theological adversaries, particularly Gregory Akindynos, who objected not to the basic hesychastic spirituality, as did Barlaam, but to the theological formulations espoused by Palamas. If God were absolutely transcendent, but also could be "experienced" and "seen" as an uncreated and real Presence, one had to speak both of a totally transcendent divine "essence" and of uncreated, but revealed, "energies." It is this famous distinction that Akindynos refused to admit: For him God was identical with His essence, and a vision of God, if it was to be admitted as a possibility, was a vision either of that divine essence itself, or of its *created* manifestations. No real distinctions were conceivable in the uncreated Being of God himself.

The civil war ended with a victory of Cantacuzenos in 1347, and by his crowning as co-emperor, sharing power with the legitimate heir, John V Palaeologus. In 1347 and, particularly, 1351, new councils endorsed the theology of Palamas, against the objections of the philosopher and historian Nicephorus Gregoras, who supported the views of Akindynos. In 1347, Gregory Palamas was elected archbishop of Thessalonica. His monastic friends and disciples—Isidore, Kallistos and Philotheus Kokkinos—successively occupied the patriarchal throne. The victory of hesychasm, as expressed not only in monastic spirituality but also in the theology of Palamas, influenced Eastern Orthodoxy as a whole, in Byzantium and throughout Eastern Europe. A generation of spiritual zealots came to positions of leadership and contributed greatly to the survival of Orthodox Christianity during the hard years of Ottoman rule in the Balkans and the Middle East. The spiritual legacy of hesychasm was also transmitted to Russia.

Gregory Palamas spent a year (1354–1355) in Asia Minor as a prisoner of the Turks, who had intercepted his boat as he was travelling between Thessalonica and the capital.[12] Ransomed by the Serbs, he returned to his episcopal see, where he died on November 14, 1359.[13]

In 1368, a decision of the Synod of Constantinople, presided over by patriarch Philotheus, proclaimed Gregory Palamas a saint. His relics are venerated to this day at the cathedral of Thessalonica.

The "Triads" for the Defence of the Holy Hesychasts

In spite of the fact that the *Triads* were written as a polemical work, directed against the position of Barlaam the Calabrian in his controversy with the hesychast monks, it represents a major witness to the content and meaning of Christian experience. The author never speaks of that experience as being individually his own. He is certainly not a representative of any form of esoteric mysticism. Quite the contrary, his intention is to formulate an objective theological foundation justifying his brothers, the hesychast monks, in their understanding of prayer and in the pursuit of their avowed goal: the deification or *theosis* of man in Christ. The main concern of Palamas is to affirm that this goal is not reserved to isolated "mystics", but is, in fact, identical with the Christian faith itself and, therefore, offered to all the members of the Church, in virtue of their baptism. It is also his contention that the entire Greek patristic tradition can be seen as an affirmation of the goal of *theosis*.

In a detailed introduction to my edition of the original Greek text of the *Triads*, I attempted to describe the circumstances and the chronology of the first encounters between Palamas and Barlaam.[14] Their correspondence began in 1336, as we saw earlier, and was initially concerned with the problem of the "apodictic" or "dialectic" knowledge of God. The logic of the debate soon led Barlaam to criticize the very notion of "spiritual knowledge" affirmed by the monks and to attack with particular virulence their method of prayer, which implied the participation of the *body* in the continuous practice of the Jesus Prayer and, consequently, in the very reality of communion with God. Some of the writings of the Calabrian philosopher used derogatory terms: The monks were "people-whose-soul-is-in-their-navel" (*omphalopsychoi*) because, following instructions of authors like Nicephorus the Hesychast, they disciplined their attention by lowering their eyes "towards the center of their bodies" and, thus, concentrated on prayer. Barlaam also affirmed that secular education, or "acquisition of wisdom", was a condition for a true knowledge of God.

Palamas began writing his first triad for "the Defence of Holy Hesychasts" on the basis of his own face-to-face discussions with Barlaam and also of some oral accounts of the philosopher's views. The name of Barlaam is not yet mentioned in this first triad. Faced with an indirect rebuttal, Barlaam softened some of his more extreme criticisms (suppressing allusions to navel watching, etc.) and published a three-part treatise: *On the Acquisition of Wisdom, On Prayer* and *On the Light of Knowledge.* The second triad of Palamas—written during a trip of Barlaam to Avignon 1339, where he unsuccessfully negotiated Church union with Pope Benedict XII—is a refutation of these treatises by the Calabrian philosopher, with direct quotations from them.

On his return to Constantinople, faced with the now public polemical exchange with a respected leader of Athonite monasticism, Barlaam published a new treatise, entitled "Against the Messalians", openly accusing his opponents of preaching the doctrine of a formally condemned sect. As we have seen earlier, the Messalians, or "Bogomils", claimed to contemplate, through prayer, the very essence of God with their material eyes. This provided Palamas with the topic of his third and last triad, where the argument concentrates on the distinction, in God, between "essence" and "energy". Disclaiming any Messalian influence, but maintaining the full reality of communion with God himself—and not only with "created grace"—Palamas develops his doctrine of the uncreated divine energies.

The debate ends with the endorsement given to Palamas, first by the whole monastic community of Mount Athos (the so-called *Tomos Haghioreitikos*) and then by the Council of Constantinople in 1341, and the emigration of Barlaam to Italy in the same year.

It can be safely said that the true message of Byzantine mediaeval hesychasm and the essential meaning of what is now generally called "palamism" is fully expressed in the *Triads.* In the course of his later life, Gregory was confronted with major political difficulties and was faced with the opposition of Akindynos and Gregoras. He wrote profusely in the form of theological letters, or lengthy treatises.[15] His theology acquired greater polemical rigidity, but no substantially new dimension was added to the vision already found in the *Triads.* However, it is not possible to acquire a full understanding of Gregory Palamas, as a person and as a churchman, without reading also his sixty-one preserved sermons, delivered when he served as archbishop of Thessalonica. Here he appears not as a polemicist, or a theologian playing with concepts, but as an accessible pastor, concerned with the spiritual and social welfare of his simple flock. This aspect of his personality is certainly as revealing of his authentically Christian experience as are his theological arguments against Barlaam, Akindynos or Nicephoros Gregoras.

Limited by the available space, but also concerned with producing an accessible and manageable volume of writings by Palamas, we are presenting here, in translation, those passages of the *Triads* that are most representative of the main thrust of his thought and his spirituality. On the other hand, anyone familiar with the style of Byzantine mediaeval literature will agree that the main defects of this literature lie in verbosity and repetitiousness, which may rebuke the modern reader. Palamas is less guilty of such flaws than some of his contemporaries because, like most monastic writers, he is less concerned than others with preserving artificial faithfulness to literary models of antiquity. Nevertheless, repetitions—sometimes required by the very polemical character of this voluminous work—are not lacking in the *Triads*, and we felt that their omission would not be a real loss.

The translation is arranged topically around major themes, which require brief introductions.

Philosophy and Salvation

One of the most striking characteristics of Byzantine mediaeval Christianity is its concern with the role of ancient Greek philosophical categories in the formulation of Christian theology and spirituality.[16] In fact, unlike their Latin contemporaries who "discovered" Greek philosophy—in Latin translations from the Arabic—in the twelfth century, the Byzantines had never forgotten Plato or Aristotle, who represented their own Greek cultural past and were always accessible to them in the original Greek text. At the same time, they always recognized that this past was a "pagan" past. Thus, the Ancient Greek heritage could still be useful in such fields as logics, physics or medicine (hence the inclusion of Aristotle in the standard Byzantine educational curriculum followed by Palamas in his youth), but not in religion. Metaphysical and religious truths could validly originate only in the Christian revelation. This is the reason that Plato and the Neoplatonists were always looked at with suspicion in conservative—and particularly monastic—circles of the Byzantine Church: Indeed, in any form of Platonic thought, no understanding of reality was possible without metaphysical, that is, in fact, theological presuppositions foreign to Christianity.

It is not astonishing, therefore, to find out that every year, on the first Sunday of Lent—also known as the "Sunday of Orthodoxy"—all Byzantine Orthodox churches resounded with formal and repeated anathemas against "those who follow the foolish opinions of the Hellenic disciplines" and particularly against those "who considered the ideas of Plato as truly existing" or believe (with Aristotle) in the eternity of matter.[17] These anathemas were first issued in the eleventh century on the occasion of the condemnation of the philosopher John Italos, but their inclusion in the liturgical *Synodikon* of the Sunday of Orthodoxy gave them permanent significance.

Clearly, however, Greek philosophical concepts were inseparable from many aspects and formulations of the patristic tradition, which was the common model and authority for all Byzantines. The repeated clashes between "humanists" who tended to minimize the prohibitions against "Hellenic wisdom" and those theologians, predominantly monastic, who insisted on the incompatibility between "Athens" and "Jerusalem" (to use the old expression of Tertullian) could not solve the issue in a definite way. Similarly, in the controversy between Barlaam and Palamas, both sides acknowledged the authority of the Christian revelation and, on the other hand, admitted that ancient philosophers possessed a certain natural ability to reach not only created, but also divine truths. What then separated them, and made the debate appear essentially a debate on the relation between ancient philosophy and the Christian experience?

On the one hand, the different backgrounds and intellectual formation of Palamas and Barlaam led them to assign to Greek philosophy a different *degree* of authority. Barlaam's contacts with Western thought and his involvement in the "humanist" milieus in Byzantium were leading him to an enthusiastic endorsement of Aristotle and Neoplatonic authors, as criteria of Christian thought. "I cannot conceive that God has not illuminated them in a certain manner, and feel that they must surpass the multitude of mankind," he wrote.[18] Palamas, on the contrary, preferred to approach the ancient Greek philosophical tradition as requiring the need for a baptismal rebirth—a death and a resurrection—as a condition for its integration into the

Tradition of the Church: This is the meaning of his image of serpents' being killed and dissected before providing materials used in helpful drugs.[19]

However, beyond this difference of taste and method one discovers a deeper and more serious conflict between the two men. Barlaam launches against the monks the somewhat superficial accusation of "ignorance", which appears at the very outset of the debate. He also contends that "God is only knowable through the mediation of His creatures".[20] Of course, Barlaam may be misrepresented by Palamas when he is accused of teaching that knowledge of God is possible *only* through creatures. The Calabrian philosopher does believe also in an illumination of the mind, which leads to a vision of the divine Being. He is familiar with—and admiring of—the writings of Ps. Dionysius and of St. Maximus the Confessor, where a direct vision of God and deification are seen as the goal of Christian life. It remains, nevertheless, that a certain "knowledge of beings" (*gnōsis tōn ontōn*) is, for Barlaam, a *condition* for illumination, and it is this conditioning that led to his conflict with the monks and that is unacceptable to Palamas. If "knowledge", identified with secular education, is necessary to know God, what is the meaning of Matthew 11:25 ("You have hidden these things from the wise and prudent and have revealed them to babes,") or of the references, so frequent in Palamas,[21] to Romans 1, or 1 Corinthians 1–2, about the "wisdom of this age" being "put to shame"?

In Palamas there is no denigration of the "knowledge of beings", and therefore no obscurantism. Furthermore, his own understanding of illumination in Christ implies that the mind, transfigured by grace, opens up also to a knowledge of creatures. Neither is there, in Palamism, a systematic opposition to secular learning. Not only is Palamas himself clearly indebted to his training in Aristotelian logics, but also his disciple and biographer, Philotheos Kokkinos, likes to embellish his writings with references to authors of antiquity. Furthermore, the triumph of Palamism in the Byzantine Church, completed in 1351, did not interrupt the development of secular humanism, which produced on the eve of Byzantium's fall such figures as Gemisthos Pletho and Bessarion.[22]

The debate between Barlaam and the hesychasts can probably be best understood in the light of their different interpretations of what St. Maximus the Confessor used to call "natural contemplation" (*physikē theōria*) or the new state of created being in Christ. Barlaam—and also mediaeval Latin tradition—tends to understand this created *habi-*

INTRODUCTION

tus as a condition for and not a consequence of illumination by grace.
Palamas, on the contrary, proclaims the overwhelming novelty of the
Kingdom of God revealed in Christ, and the gratuitous character of
the divine and saving acts of God. Hence, for him, vision of God cannot depend on human "knowledge." Of course, in Greek patristic terminology, and particularly in St. Maximus, "nature" presupposes
divine presence in man, that is, "grace". No opposition between "nature" and "grace" is therefore possible.[23] But salvation itself begins
by a divine act providing direct knowledge of God, which restores
"nature" to its original state and also allows for a truly "natural" contemplation of God through His creatures. Palamas always remains
basically faithful to the thought of St. Maximus who, together with
Ps. Dionysius, is the patristic author most frequently quoted in the
Triads.

Knowledge beyond Knowledge

The philosopher Barlaam's debate with Palamas on the subject of
Greek philosophy and its relevance to Christian thought had inevita-
bly to confront the nature of Christian experience itself, which was
described by Palamas as being "beyond nature". Barlaam, on the contrary, seems to have clung to the Aristotelian approach, defining all
human knowledge as being based on perception *by the senses,* also ad-
mitting the possibility of a positive illumination of the mind, transcending the senses, but remaining within "the nature of the mind".
Of course, Barlaam also knew the apophatic or "negative" theology of
the Greek Fathers, and particularly Ps. Dionysius, but he used this
theology mainly to maintain the limitations of the human mind,
whose knowledge of God, according to Barlaam, could be only symbolic, or relative. Indeed, the meaning of negative theology consists
precisely in saying only what *God is not,* but not what *He is.*[24]

In the texts translated below in Section B, Palamas argues that
"God is not only beyond knowledge, but also beyond unknowing".

Both protagonists clearly agreed on the central role of the *via negativa,* in Christian theology, as an expression of God's transcendence. The writings of the Fathers—and particularly Dionysius—
emphasized, as the starting point of any Christian discourse about
God, the affirmation that God is not any of the creatures and that,
therefore, the created mind, which "knows" only creatures, can conceive of God only by the method of exclusion. The most frequently

13

repeated liturgical prayers, familiar to all, were using the same apophatic approach to God: "Thou art God ineffable, invisible, incomprehensible", proclaimed the preface of the Eucharistic canon of the
liturgy celebrated in all the churches. According to the Fathers, this
transcendence of God was experienced by Moses when he entered the
cloud on the top of Mount Sinai and perceived the presence of God in
the darkness of unknowing.

However, the major point made by Palamas in his *Triads* is precisely that the darkness of the cloud surrounding God is not an empty
darkness. While eliminating all perceptions of the senses, or of the
mind, it nevertheless places man before a Presence, revealed to a
transfigured mind and a purified body. Thus, divine "unknowability
does not mean agnosticism, or refusal to know God", but is a preliminary step for "a change of heart and mind enabling us to attain to the
contemplation of the reality which reveals itself to us as it raises us to
God".[25]

In other words, true knowledge of God implies a transfiguration
of man by the Spirit of God, and the negations of apophatic theology
signify only the inability of reaching God without such a transfiguration by the Spirit.

This approach to the issue of the experience of God implies, in
Palamas, both a basic anthropological presupposition and a theological principle.

The anthropological presupposition is that man is capable of
transcending his own nature, that, being created according to the image
of God, he posseses "an organ of vision" that is "neither the senses,
nor the intellect" (p. 35). He is admitted to "true vision" when he
"ceases to see" (p. 38). We will see below—in connection with the
Christological views of Palamas—that this capacity of transcending
oneself is always understood personalistically: The person (or hypostasis), in virtue of its freedom (which *is* the image of God, according
to St. Gregory of Nyssa), possesses an *openness*, a capacity *to love* the
other and therefore, particularly, to love God, and to know Him in
love.

The theological principle presupposed by Palamas is that God,
even when He communicates Himself to the purified body and mind,
remains transcendent in His essence. In this, Palamas follows St. Gregory of Nyssa, who spoke of mystical experience in terms of an experience of divine inexhaustibility, and used the term *tension (epektasis)* to
describe it: Communion with God never becomes exhaustion or satu-

ration, but implies the revelation that greater things are always to come. The model of the Song of Songs inspires the mystics in describing union with God as a limitless ascent "from glory to glory", similar to a perfect form of erotic love, in which true joy is, at the same time, fulfillment and further expectation.

Thus, apophatic theology is much more than a simple dialectical device to ascertain the transcendence of God in terms of human logic. It also describes a state, beyond the conceptual process, where God reveals himself positively to the "spiritual senses", without losing anything of His transcendence, as "light", as "source of deification", while remaining "more-than-God", and "more-than-Principle" (p. 39). This is what leads Palamas to his distinction between the ultimately transcendent and unknowable essence of God on the one hand, and, on the other, the deifying and uncreated energies through which man enters in communion with the Unknowable.

The Transfigured Body

Throughout the centuries, Christian spirituality has often been influenced by Platonic terminology and ideas, which tended to describe the fallen state of man in terms of an opposition between spirit and matter. For Origen and Evagrius, the ultimate goal of prayer and contemplation is for the mind to become "free from all matter".[26] This spiritualistic and intellectual trend in spirituality was familiar to Barlaam, who, on the other hand, had no taste for the more sacramental and more biblical anthropology, connected with the writings of Ps. Macarius. He was even less able to appreciate the spiritual methods, or exercises, that appear in texts of the late thirteenth century (although they are certainly more ancient in origin), and that aim at reestablishing the unity of spirit and body, as a single psychosomatic organism, in the act of prayer.

Two such methods, very similar in content, are formally referred to by Palamas in the *Triads*.[27] The first, by an unknown author, is attributed to St. Symeon the New Theologian.[28] The second is by the Hesychast Nicephorus, an Italian who became a monk on Mount Athos during the reign of Michael VIII Palaeologus (1259–1282).[29] As one can see from the following excerpt from Nicephorus, they describe a breathing discipline, aimed at acquiring permanent "vigilance" in prayer, and presupposing that the *heart* is the vital center of psychosomatic life.

15

You know that we breathe our breath in and out, only because of our heart ... so, as I have said, sit down, recollect your mind, draw it—I am speaking of your mind—in your nostrils; that is the path the breath takes to reach the heart. Drive it, force it to go down to your heart with the air you are breathing in. When it is there, you will see the joy that follows: you will have nothing to regret. As a man who has been away from home for a long time cannot restrain his joy at seeing his wife and children again, so the spirit overflows with joy and unspeakable delights when it is united again to the soul.

Next you must know that as long as your spirit abides there, you must not remain silent nor idle. Have no other occupation or meditation than the cry of: "Lord Jesus Christ, Son of God, have mercy on me!" Under no circumstances give yourself any rest. This practice protects your spirit from wandering and makes it impregnable and inaccessible to the suggestions of the enemy and lifts it up every day in love and desire for God.[30]

We do not know for sure whether Barlaam met hesychasts who applied this rather simple breathing technique literally, or whether he witnessed naive or superstitious abuses. In any case, his stand against the practice was unambiguous. He called the monks *omphalopsychoi*—"people-whose-soul-is-in-their-navel"—and protested the principle that the body can or should participate in "pure prayer".

The reaction of Palamas—as reflected in the texts of Section C below, which represent the most direct and self-explanatory sections of the *Triads*—is to refer to the human body as the natural "temple of the Holy Spirit which is in us" (1 Cor. 6:19). He is unconcerned with the various physiological views about the location of the mind in the brain or the heart, but tends to prefer the Macarian concept of the heart as the main "instrument" of the Spirit. His biblical references all point to the actions of God on and through the material and fleshly side of man, as well as through the soul, and in opposition to the platonic dualism between spirit and matter. His implications are also sacramental: Baptism and Eucharistic communion sanctify the whole man. Why not accept and encourage the participation of the body in prayer?

INTRODUCTION

As we have seen in connection with the treatment of apophatic theology by Palamas, God transcends creatures as such, not the human body or mind in particular. Thus, His revelation of His presence and of His Sanctifying Spirit touches both the spiritual and physical sides of man. Without this presence and this sanctification no real communion with God is possible.

Deification and the Uncreated Glory of Christ

In his theological defense of hesychasm, Palamas is particularly concerned with one possible misunderstanding: the identification of the Christian experience with either intellectual knowledge, or any form of physical, or mystical—but *natural*—vision. As we have seen earlier, he does not deny relative achievements of Greek philosophy, or the participation of natural human functions, such as the body or the "heart", in perceiving divine Presence. However, the Presence itself is not the simple result of "natural" efforts, whether intellectual, or ascetical, but is the gift of personal divine communion, or deification (*theōsis*) that transcends all creatures. It is "uncreated", because it is the self-giving God Himself. It is a "hypostatic" light, "seen spiritually by the saints", that "exists not symbolically only, as do manifestations produced by fortuitous events", but is "an illumination immaterial and divine, a grace invisibly seen and ignorantly known. What it is, they do not pretend to know" (p. 57).

In the context of this affirmation of God's real manifestation to creatures, Palamas, following Maximus the Confessor and John of Damascus, refers to the New Testament accounts and references to the Transfiguration of Christ on the mount (Mt. 17:1–9; Mk. 9:2–9; Lk. 9:28–36; 2 Pet. 1:17–21). And since the mount of Transfiguration is traditionally identified with Mount Thabor, the whole debate between Barlaam and Palamas is frequently referred to as the controversy on the "thaboric light". And indeed in Greek patristic tradition, since Origen and St. Gregory of Nyssa, the vision of God is always defined as a luminous vision, probably because the central biblical (and particularly Johannine) theme of "light" and "darkness" was also familiar to Neoplatonists, and could easily serve as a convenient theological model. However, one of the major concerns of Palamas is to draw a sharp distinction between any form of light-experience outside of the Christian revelation, and the real vision of

INTRODUCTION

God as Light that appeared to the disciples on the mount of Transfiguration and that, in Christ, has become accessible to the members of His Body, the Church. Indeed, true "deification" (*theōsis*) became possible when, according to the expression of St. Athanasius, "God became man in order that man might become God in him."[31] Consequently, according to Palamas, a radical change intervened after the Incarnation in the relationship between God and man, which leaves all other experiences and discoveries—either in the Old Testament or among the Greeks—as mere shadows of the realities to come. He writes: "Deification would have belonged to all nations even before (Christ) came if it naturally pertains to the rational soul, just as today it would belong to everyone irrespective of faith or piety" (p. 85).

This does not imply, however, that Palamas understands deification in Augustinian terms, implying a strict opposition between "nature" and "grace." As has been shown by many modern historians, Greek patristic anthropology is "theocentric".

At his creation, man was endowed with some "divine characteristics" in that he is God's "image and likeness". According to St. Maximus the Confessor, these characteristics are "being" and "eternity" (which God possesses by nature, but gives also to man),[32] and, earlier, St. Irenaeus of Lyons identified the "spirit" naturally belonging to man with the Holy Spirit.[33] Consequently, man is not fully man unless he is in communion with God: He is "open upwards" and destined to share God's fellowship.[34] However, because God remains absolutely transcendent in His essence, man's communion with Him has no limit. It never reaches an End, which would be a dead end. God is both transcendent and inexhaustible. Man's communion with Him can never be "closed" through exhaustion. This is the transcendence that Palamas defends, and sees as the most central, the most positive and the most essential aspect not only of hesychasm, as a tradition of monastic spirituality, but as a basic element of the Christian faith as such: In Christ, man enters in communion not with "the God of the philosophers and the savants", but the One who—in human language—can only be called "more-than-God".

Hypostatically, "personally," the Logos—second Person of the Trinity—by assuming the fulness of humanity, became in His Body the source or locus of deification. Being "deified" means "being in Him", that is, participant of His Body, which is penetrated (in virtue of the "communication of idioms" in the hypostatic union)[35] with divine life, or "energy". The Eucharistic communion in the deified humanity of Christ, in the form of Bread and Wine, has precisely this meaning. Here is an often-quoted passage of Palamas on this crucial issue:

> Since the Son of God, in his incomparable love for man, did not only unite His divine Hypostasis with our nature, by clothing Himself in a living body and a soul gifted with intelligence . . . but also united himself . . . with the human hypostases themselves, in mingling himself with each of the faithful by communion with his Holy Body, and since he becomes one single body with us (cf. Eph. 3:6), and makes us a temple of the undivided Divinity, for in the very body of Christ dwelleth the fulness of the Godhead bodily (Col. 2:9), how should he not illuminate those who commune worthily with the divine ray of His Body which is within us, lightening their souls, as He illumined the very bodies of the disciples on Mount Thabor? For, on the day of the Transfiguration, that Body, source of the light of grace, was not yet united with our bodies; it illuminated from outside those who worthily approached it, and sent the illumination into the soul by the intermediary of the physical eyes; but now, since it is mingled with us and exists in us, it illuminates the soul from within.[36]

It is precisely because Palamas understands illumination in the framework of Orthodox Christology that he insists on the *uncreated* character of divine light: This uncreated light is the very divinity of Christ, shining through his humanity. If Christ is truly God, this light is authentically divine. The same Christological framework makes it inevitable to distinguish between the transcendent essence, or nature of God, and His energies. Indeed, in Christ, His two natures—so precisely defined at Chalcedon as both "inseparable" and "unconfused"—remain distinct. Therefore, deification or communion between divinity and humanity does not imply a confusion of essences or natures. It remains nevertheless *real* communion between the Uncreated and His creature, and real deification—not by essence, but by *energy*. The humanity of Christ, "enhypostasized" by the Logos, is penetrated with divine energy, and Christ's body becomes the source of divine light and deification. It is "theurgic", that is, it communicates divine life to those who are "in Christ" and participate in the uncreated energies active in it.

Another aspect of the Christian experience, particularly important in monastic spirituality as described by Palamas, is its eschatological character. The reference to the Second Epistle of Peter 1, where the episode of the Transfiguration of Christ is interpreted as "confirming the prophetic word", appears repeatedly in the *Triads*. It places the hesychast spirituality in the context of the biblical notion of "prophecy", which in the Old Testament implied an anticipated vision of the Messianic age, realized in Christ, and still remains in the New Testament an experience by "the Saints" of the Age to Come.[37] However, whereas the Old Testament prophets perceived only a symbolic anticipation of the Kingdom, the New Testament Church founded on sacramental communion and "life in Christ" offers a participation in the very reality of the divine life. Granted to all the baptized, this participation is personal and conscious: It happens in the "heart" of the saints.

Essence and Energies of God

The distinction in God between "essence" and "energy"—that focal point of Palamite theology—is nothing but a way of saying that the transcendent God remains transcendent, as He also communicates Himself to humanity.

The distinction, which was officially endorsed by the Orthodox Church at a series of councils in the fourteenth century, has been a topic of debate and controversy. It is obviously impossible to present here all the elements of the debate.[38] I will limit myself to a few simple remarks that will allow the reader to understand better an affirmation that appears repeatedly in the *Triads,* and is more specifically developed in texts of *Triad III,* translated in Section F below.

Having initially attacked the hesychast monks for their claim to possess a real experience and vision of God—which he himself tended to consider either as a mystical illumination of the mind, or a symbol, or an aberration—Barlaam the Calabrian, facing oral and written rebukes, published a book entitled *Against the Messalians.* By identifying the monks as Messalians, a condemned charismatic sect, he was accusing them of pretending "to contemplate the essence of God with their physical eyes". It was, therefore, inevitable for Palamas to recall the apophatic theology of the Greek Fathers, which affirmed absolute transcendence of the divine essence, inaccessible to the angels themselves.

However, for Palamas, this transcendent essence of God would be a philosophical abstraction if it did not possess "power", that is, "the faculties of knowing, of prescience, of creating" (p. 93). In other words, the God of Palamas is a living God, ultimately indescribable in the categories of essentialist Greek philosophy. He says so much himself, referring to the revelation of the divine Name to Moses on Mount Sinai: "When God was conversing with Moses," writes Palamas, "He did not say, 'I am the essence,' but 'I am the One Who is' (Ex. 3:14). Thus, it is not the One Who is Who derives from the essence, but essence that derives from Him, for it is He Who contains all being in Himself" (p. 98).

The real communion, the fellowship and—one can almost say—the familiarity with the "One Who is" is, for Palamas, the very content of the Christian experience, made possible because the One Who is became man. It is this familiarity with and immediate communion with God that was at stake, according to Palamas, in his debate with Barlaam. For Barlaam, God was identical with His essence, and there was no real possibility for man to be in communion with divine essence: "Illumination" conceived as a created state was, however, accessible, but through a mediation of the angelic hierarchies. On this point, Barlaam was undoubtedly referring to the famous writings of Ps. Dionysius the Areopagite, who viewed God-man relationships as a scale of mediations—the "celestial" and the "ecclesiastical" hierarchies—a Christian version of the Neoplatonic world system. Palamas rejected this approach with indignation. Of course, he respected the writings of Ps. Dionysius, whom he counted among the greatest Fathers of the Church, but he took the "hierarchies" of Dionysius, as describing the relationships between God and man, as they existed in the Old Testament, when God was speaking only "through angels" (Heb. 2:2).[39] After the coming of Christ, however, God enters into immediate communion with humanity. "Did He not deign to make His dwelling in man", asks Palamas, "to appear to him and speak to him without intermediary, so that man should be not only pious, but sanctified and purified in advance in soul and body by keeping the divine commandments, and so be transformed into a vehicle worthy to receive the all-powerful Spirit?"

So, communion with God in Christ is real and immediate. It is not pantheistic absorption into the Divine however: Man, being "in

INTRODUCTION

God", or rather "in Christ", preserves his full humanity, his freedom (he is required to "keep the commandments"), and he participates in a process that knows no end, because God, in His transcendent essence, is always "above" any given experience of Him. But man's communion is not with "created grace" only, but with God Himself. This is the meaning of the doctrine of the "uncreated energies", which, as we have seen earlier in this Introduction, is rooted in the Christological doctrine of "hypostatic union" as it was formulated in the East after Chalcedon particularly by St. Maximus the Confessor.

The doctrine of the energies was defined with ever greater refinement in the later writings of Palamas, particularly those he directed against Gregory Akindynos in 1342–1347. But in order to understand these conceptual and frequently polemical definitions, the initial freshness of his debate with Barlaam, as it is found in the *Triads,* is always to be remembered as the necessary context of Palamite theology. The only concern of Palamas was to affirm simultaneously the transcendence of God and His immanence in the free gift of communion in the Body of Christ. This concern could not be fully expressed in philosophical or conceptual terms. In maintaining it, Palamas is neither an innovator nor a blind conservative, but, as an authentic spokesman for the Greek patristic tradition, he never lost sense of the tension and the polarity between Greek thought and the Christian gospel. It is this sense that opposes him to his theological critics, old and new.

Gregory Palamas

The Triads

Translator's Note
The titles of the five sections of texts, numbered A, B, C, D, and E have been added by the Editor. The chapter numbers refer to Meyendorff's edition of the *Triads*.

A. Philosophy does not save

I. i. The first question

I[1] have heard it stated by certain people that monks also should pursue secular wisdom, and that if they do not possess this wisdom, it is impossible for them to avoid ignorance and false opinions, even if they have achieved the highest level of impassibility;[2] and that one cannot acquire perfection and sanctity without seeking knowledge from all quarters, above all from Greek culture,[3] which also is a gift of God—just as were those insights granted to the prophets and apostles through revelation. This education confers on the soul the knowledge of [created] beings,[4] and enriches the faculty of knowledge, which is the greatest of all the powers of the soul. For education not only dispels all other evils from the soul—since every passion has its root and foundation in ignorance—but it also leads men to the knowledge of God, for God is knowable only through the mediation of His creatures.[5]

I was in no way convinced when I heard such views being put forward, for my small experience of monastic life showed me that just the opposite was the case; but I was unable to make a defence against them. "We not only occupy ourselves with the mysteries of nature," they proudly claimed, "measuring the celestial cycle, and studying the opposed motions of the stars, their conjunctions, phases and risings, and reckoning the consequences of these things (in all of which matters we take great pride); but in addition, since the inner principles of these phenomena are to be found in the divine and primordial creative Mind, and the images of these principles exist in our soul, we are zealous to understand them, and to cast off every kind of igno-

25

rance in their regard by the methods of distinction, syllogistic reason-ing and analysis; thus, both in this life and after, we wish to be conformed to the likeness of the Creator."[6]

I felt myself incapable of responding to these arguments, and so maintained silence towards these men; but now I beg you, Father, to instruct me in what should be said in defence of the truth, so that (fol-lowing the Apostle's injunction) I may "be ready to give an account of the faith that is in us".[7]

I. i. 18.

By examining the nature of sensible things,[8] these people[9] have arrived at a certain concept of God, but not at a conception truly wor-thy of Him and appropriate to His blessed nature. For their "disor-dered heart was darkened" by the machinations of the wicked demons who were instructing them. For if a worthy conception of God could be attained through the use of intellection, how could these people have taken the demons for gods, and how could they have believed the demons when they taught man polytheism?[10] In this way, wrapped up in this mindless and foolish wisdom and unen-lightened education, they have calumniated both God and nature. They have deprived God of His sovereignty (at least as far as they are concerned); they have ascribed the Divine Name to demons; and they were so far from finding the knowledge of beings—the object of their desire and zeal—as to claim that inanimate things have a soul and par-ticipate in a soul superior to our own.[12] They also allege that things without reason are reasonable, since capable of receiving a human soul; that demons are superior to us and are even our creators (such is their impiety); they have classed among things uncreated and unori-ginate and coeternal with God, not only matter, and what they call the World Soul, but also those intelligible beings not clothed in the opacity of the body,[13] and even our souls themselves.[14]

Are we then to say that those who hold such a philosophy possess the wisdom of God, or even a human wisdom in general? I hope that none of us would be so mad as to claim this, for, as the Lord declared, "A good tree does not produce bad fruit" (Mt. 7:18). In my estimation, this "wisdom" is not even worthy of the appellation "human", since it is so inconsistent as to affirm the same things to be at once animate and inanimate, endowed with and deprived of reason, and it holds that things by nature without sensibility, and having no organs capa-

ble of sensation, could contain our souls![15] It is true that Paul sometimes speaks of this as "human wisdom", as when he says, "My
proclamation does not rest on the persuasive words of human wisdom",[16] and again, "We do not speak in words which teach human
wisdom."[17] But at the same time, he thinks it right to call those who
have acquired it "wise according to the flesh",[18] or "wise men become
feebleminded",[19] "the disputants of this age",[20] and their wisdom is
qualified by him in similar terms: It is "wisdom become folly",[21] the
"wisdom which has been done away",[22] "vain trumpery",[23] the "wisdom of this age", and belongs to the "princes" of this age—who are
"coming to an end".[24]

19

For myself, I listen to the father who[25] says, "Woe to body when
it does not consume the nourishment that is from without, and woe to
the soul when it does not receive the grace that is from above!" He
speaks justly—for the body will perish once it has passed into the
world of inanimate things, and the soul will become enmeshed in the
demonic life and the thoughts of demons if it turns away from that
which is proper to it.[26]

But if one says that philosophy, insofar as it is natural, is a gift of
God, then one says true, without contradiction, and without incur-
ring the accusation that falls on those who abuse philosophy and pervert it to an unnatural end.[27] Indeed they make their condemnation
heavier by using God's gift in a way unpleasing to Him.

Moreover, the mind of demons, created by God, possesses by nature its faculty of reason. But we do not hold that its activity comes
from God, even though its possibility of acting comes from Him; one
could with propriety call such reason an unreason. The intellect of
pagan philosophers is likewise a divine gift insofar as it naturally possesses a wisdom endowed with reason. But it has been perverted by
the wiles of the devil, who has transformed it into a foolish wisdom,
wicked and senseless, since it puts forward such doctrines.

But if someone tells us that the demons themselves have a desire
and knowledge not absolutely bad, since they desire to exist, live and
think, here is the proper reply which I should give: It is not right to
take issue with us because we say (with the brother of the Lord) that
Greek wisdom is "demonic",[28] on the grounds that it arouses quarrels
and contains almost every kind of false teaching, and is alienated from
its proper end, that is, the knowledge of God; but at the same time

recognise that it may have some participation in the good in a remote and inchoate manner.[29] It should be remembered that no evil thing is evil insofar as it exists, but insofar as it is turned aside from the activity appropriate to it, and thus from the end assigned to this activity.

20

What then should be the work and the goal of those who seek the wisdom of God in creatures? Is it not the acquisition of the truth, and the glorification of the Creator? This is clear to all. But the knowledge of the pagan philosophers has fallen away from both these aims.

Is there then anything of use to us in this philosophy? Certainly. For just as there is much therapeutic value even in substances obtained from the flesh of serpents,[30] and the doctors consider there is no better and more useful medicine than that derived from this source, so there is something of benefit to be had even from the profane philosophers—but somewhat as in a mixture of honey and hemlock. So it is most needful that those who wish to separate out the honey from the mixture should beware that they do not take the deadly residue by mistake. And if you were to examine the problem, you would see that all or most of the harmful heresies derive their origin from this source.

It is thus with the "iconognosts", who pretend that man receives the image of God by knowledge, and that this knowledge conforms the soul to God.[31] For, as was said to Cain, "If you make your offering correctly, without dividing correctly...".[32] But to divide well is the property of very few men. Those alone "divide well", the senses of whose souls[33] are trained to distinguish good and evil.

What need is there to run these dangers without necessity, when it is possible to contemplate the wisdom of God in His creatures not only without peril but with profit? A life which hope in God has liberated from every care naturally impels the soul towards the contemplation of God's creatures. Then it is struck with admiration, deepens its understanding, persists in the glorification of the Creator, and through this sense of wonder is led forward to what is greater. According to St. Isaac,[34] "It comes upon treasures which cannot be expressed in words"; and using prayer as a key, it penetrates thereby into the mysteries[35] which "eye has not seen, ear has not heard and which have not entered into the heart of man",[36] mysteries manifested by the Spirit alone to those who are worthy, as St. Paul teaches.

28

21

Do you see the swiftest way, full of profit and without danger, that leads to these supernatural and heavenly treasures?

In the case of the secular wisdom, you must first kill the serpent, in other words, overcome the pride that arises from this philosophy. How difficult that is! "The arrogance of philosophy has nothing in common with humility", as the saying goes. Having overcome it, then, you must separate and cast away the head and tail, for these things are evil in the highest degree. By the head, I mean manifestly wrong opinions concerning things intelligible and divine and primordial; and by the tail, the fabulous stories concerning created things. As to what lies in between the head and tail, that is, discourses on nature, you must separate out useless ideas by means of the faculties of examination and inspection possessed by the soul, just as pharmacists purify the flesh of serpents with fire and water. Even if you do all this, and make good use of what has been properly set aside, how much trouble and circumspection will be required for the task!

Nonetheless, if you put to good use that part of the profane wisdom which has been well excised, no harm can result, for it will naturally have become an instrument for good. But even so, it cannot in the strict sense be called a gift of God[37] and a spiritual thing, for it pertains to the order of nature and is not sent from on high. This is why Paul, who is so wise in divine matters, calls it "carnal";[38] for, says he, "Consider that among us who have been chosen, there are not many wise according to the flesh".[39] For who could make better use of this wisdom than those whom Paul calls "wise from outside"?[40] But having this wisdom in mind, he calls them "wise according to the flesh", and rightly too.

22

Just as in legal marriage, the pleasure derived from procreation cannot exactly be called a gift of God, because it is carnal and constitutes a gift of nature and not of grace (even though that nature has been created by God); even so the knowledge that comes from profane education, even if well used, is a gift of nature, and not of grace—a gift which God accords to all without exception through nature, and which one can develop by exercise. This last point—that no one acquires it without effort and exercise—is an evident proof that it is a question of a natural, not a spiritual, gift.

It is our sacred wisdom that should legitimately be called a gift of God and not a natural gift, since even simple fishermen who receive it from on high become, as Gregory the Theologian says,[41] sons of Thunder, whose word has encompassed the very bounds of the universe. By this grace, even publicans are made merchants of souls; and even the burning zeal of persecutors is transformed, making them Pauls instead of Sauls,[42] turning away from the earth to attain "the third heaven" and "hear ineffable things".[43] By this true wisdom we too can become conformed to the image of God and continue to be such after death.

As to natural wisdom, it is said that even Adam possessed it in abundance, more so than all his descendents, although he was the first who failed to safeguard conformity to the image. Profane philosophy existed as an aid to this natural wisdom before the advent of Him who came to recall the soul to its ancient beauty: Why then were we not renewed by this philosophy before Christ's coming? Why did we need, not someone to teach us philosophy—an art which passes away with this age, so that it is said to be "of this age"[44]—but One "who takes away the sin of the world",[45] and who grants us a true and eternal wisdom—even though this appears as "foolishness"[46] to the ephemeral and corrupt wise men of this world, whereas in reality its absence makes truly foolish those not spiritually attached to it? Do you not clearly see that it is not the study of profane sciences which brings salvation, which purifies the cognitive faculty of the soul, and conforms it to the divine Archetype?

This, then, is my conclusion: If a man who seeks to be purified by fulfilling the prescriptions of the Law gains no benefit from Christ—even though the Law had been manifestly promulgated by God—then neither will the acquisition of the profane sciences avail. For how much more will Christ be of no benefit to one who turns to the discredited alien philosophy to gain purification for his soul? It is Paul, the mouthpiece of Christ, who tells us this and gives us his testimony.

B. Apophatic theology as positive experience

I understand better now, Father, how it is that the accusers of the hesychasts not only lack the knowledge that comes from works, and are even ignorant of that which comes from the experience of life, which alone is certain and irrefutable; they also absolutely refuse to listen to the words of the Fathers. "Puffed up with pride, they busy carnal minds with things that they have not seen",[1] as the Apostle says. They are so far from the right way that, while openly calumniating the saints, they are not even in accord with each other. Thus, in undertaking to speak of illumination, they consider any illumination which is accessible to the senses as illusion, but yet themselves affirm that all divine illumination is accessible to the senses. For they claim that all illuminations that occurred among the Jews and their prophets under the Old Law and before the coming of Christ were only symbolic; but that the illumination on Thabor at the time of the Saviour's Transfiguration, and the one when the Holy Spirit descended, and all similar phenomena, were clearly perceptible to the senses.[2] According to them, knowledge is the only illumination that transcends the senses, and so they declare it to be superior to the divine light, and the goal of all contemplation.

I shall now briefly describe to you what they claim they have heard certain people say.[3] I beg you to be patient with me, and bear in mind that I myself have never heard anything of this sort from any hesychasts. I cannot persuade myself that they could have heard such things from one of our people. They say that they pretended to be-

31

come disciples of certain monks without accepting their teaching, and wrote down what these teachers said in order to cajole and persuade them.[4] Thus, according to them, these masters suggested they should entirely abandon Sacred Scripture as something evil, and attach themselves to prayer alone: for it is prayer that drives away the evil spirits which become mingled with the very being of man. They said also that these monks become inflamed in a sensible manner, leap about and are filled with feelings of joy, without their souls being in any way changed. They see sensible lights, and come to think that the sign of divine things is a white colour, and of evil things a fiery yellow.[5]

They [the anti-hesychasts] write that those who taught them speak thus: but for their own part, they declare that all this is of the devil; and if anyone contradicts them on any point, they say this is a sign of passion, which in turn is a mark of error.[6] They throw numerous reproaches in the faces of their adversaries; in their writings they imitate the many convolutions and perfidies of the serpent, turning back upon themselves in many ways, employing many ruses, and interpreting their own words in different and contradictory manners. They do not possess the firmness and simplicity of truth, but fall easily into contradiction. Ashamed at the accusation of their own conscience, they seek like Adam to hide themselves in complication, conundrums and ambiguities about different meanings of words. I therefore beseech you, Father, to clarify our opinion on their views.

I. iii. 4.

The human mind also, and not only the angelic, transcends itself, and by victory over the passions acquires an angelic form.[7] It, too, will attain to that light[8] and will become worthy of a supernatural vision of God, not seeing the divine essence, but seeing God by a revelation appropriate and analogous to Him. One sees, not in a negative way—for one does see something—but in a manner superior to negation. For God is not only beyond knowledge, but also beyond unknowing;[9] His revelation itself is also truly a mystery of a most divine and an extraordinary kind, since the divine manifestations, even if symbolic, remain unknowable by reason of their transcendence. They appear, in fact, according to a law which is not appropriate to either human or divine nature—being, as it were, for us yet beyond us—so that no name can properly describe them. And this God indicated when, in reply to Manoe's question, "What is your name?", He replied, "It is marvellous";[10] for that vision, being not only incomprehensible but also unnameable, is no less wonderful. However, although vision be beyond negation, yet the words used to explain it are inferior to the negative way. Such explanations proceed by use of examples or analogies, and this is why the word "like", pointing to a simile, appears so often in theological discourse; for the vision itself is ineffable, and surpasses all expression.

5

So, when the saints contemplate this divine light within themselves, seeing it by the divinising communion of the Spirit, through the mysterious visitation of perfecting illuminations—then they behold the garment of their deification, their mind being glorified and filled by the grace of the Word, beautiful beyond measure in His splendour;[11] just as the divinity of the Word on the mountain glorified with divine light the body conjoined to it. For "the glory which the Father gave Him", He Himself has given to those obedient to Him, as the Gospel says, and "He willed that they should be with Him and contemplate His glory".[12]

How can this be accomplished corporeally, now that He Himself is no longer corporeally present after His ascension to the heavens? It is necessarily carried out in a spiritual fashion, for the mind becomes supercelestial, and as it were the companion of Him who passed beyond the heavens for our sake, since it is manifestly yet mysteriously united to God, and contemplates supernatural and ineffable visions, being filled with all the immaterial knowledge of a higher light. Then it is no longer the sacred symbols accessible to the senses that it contemplates, nor yet the variety of Sacred Scripture that it knows; it is made beautiful by the creative and primordial Beauty, and illumined by the radiance of God.[13]

In the same way, according to the revealer and interpreter of their hierarchy,[14] the ranks of supracosmic spirits above are hierarchically filled, in a way analogous to themselves, not only with the first-given knowledge and understanding, but with the first light in respect of the sublimest triadic initiation. Not only do they [the angels] participate in, and contemplate, the glory of the Trinity, but they likewise behold the manifestation of the light of Jesus, revealed to His disciples on Thabor.[15] Judged worthy of this vision, they are initiated into Him, for He is Himself deifying light: They truly draw

33

near to Him, and enjoy direct participation in His divinising rays. This is why the blessed Macarius calls this light "the food of the supracelestial beings".[16] And here is what another theologian says: "All the intelligible array of supracosmic beings, immaterially celebrating this light, give us a perfect proof of the love which the Word bears towards us."[17] And the great Paul, at the moment of encountering the invisible and supracelestial visions that are in Christ, was "ravished"[18] and became himself supracelestial, without his mind needing to pass beyond the heavens by actually changing place. This "ravishment" denotes a mystery of an entirely different order, known only to those who have experienced it. But it is not necessary to mention that we ourselves have heard the testimony of Fathers who have had this experience, so as not to expose these things to calumny. But what has already been said should suffice to demonstrate easily to the unconvinced that there is indeed an intellectual illumination, visible to those whose hearts have been purified, and utterly different from knowledge, though productive of it.

17

... No one has ever seen the fulness of this divine Beauty, and this is why, according to Gregory of Nyssa,[19] no eye has seen it, even if it gaze forever: In fact, it does not see the totality such as it is, but only in the measure in which it is rendered receptive to the power of the Holy Spirit. But in addition to this incomprehensibility, what is most divine and extraordinary is that the very comprehension a man may have, he possesses incomprehensibly. Those who see, in fact, do not know the one who enables them to see, hear and be initiated into knowledge of the future, or experience of eternal things, for the Spirit by whom they see is incomprehensible.[20] As the great Denys says, "Such a union of those divinised with the light that comes from on high takes place by virtue of a cessation of all intellectual activity."[21] It is not the product of a cause or a relationship, for these are dependent upon the activity of the intellect, but it comes to be by abstraction, without itself being that abstraction.[22] If it were simply abstraction, it would depend on us, and this is the Messalian doctrine, "to mount as far as one wills into the ineffable mysteries of God", as St. Isaac[23] says of these heretics.

Contemplation, then, is not simply abstraction and negation; it is a union and a divinisation which occurs mystically and ineffably by the grace of God, after the stripping away of everything from here below which imprints itself on the mind, or rather after the cessation of all intellectual activity; it is something which goes beyond abstraction (which is only the outward mark of the cessation).

This is why every believer has to separate off God from all His creatures, for the cessation of all intellectual activity and the resulting union with the light from on high is an experience and a divinising end, granted solely to those who have purified their hearts and received grace. And what am I to say of this union, when the brief vision itself is manifested only to chosen disciples, disengaged by ecstasy[24] from all perception of the senses or intellect, admitted to the true vision because they have ceased to see, and endowed with supernatural senses by their submission to unknowing? But we intend to show later on, by God's aid, that though they have indeed seen, yet their organ of vision was, properly speaking, neither the senses nor the intellect.

18

Do you now understand that in place of the intellect, the eyes and ears, they acquire the incomprehensible Spirit and by Him hear, see and comprehend? For if all their intellectual activity has stopped, how could the angels and angelic men see God except by the power of the Spirit? This is why their vision is not a sensation, since they do not receive it through the senses; nor is it intellection, since they do not find it through thought or the knowledge that comes thereby, but after the cessation of all mental activity. It is not, therefore, the product of either imagination or reason; it is neither an opinion nor a conclusion reached by syllogistic argument.

On the other hand, the mind does not acquire it simply by elevating itself through negation. For, according to the teaching of the Fathers, every divine command and every sacred law has as its final limit purity of heart; every mode and aspect of prayer reaches its term in pure prayer;[25] and every concept which strives from below towards the One Who transcends all and is separated from all comes to a halt once detached from all created beings. However, it is erroneous to say that over and above the accomplishment of the divine commands, there is nothing but purity of heart. There *are* other things, and many of them: There is the pledge of things promised in this life, and also the blessings of the life to come, which are rendered visible and accessible by this purity of heart. Thus, beyond prayer, there is the ineffable vision, and ecstasy in the vision, and the hidden mysteries. Similarly, beyond the stripping away of beings, or rather after the cessation [of our perceiving or thinking of them] accomplished not only in words, but in reality, there remains an unknowing which is beyond knowledge; though indeed a darkness, it is yet beyond radiance, and, as the great Denys says,[26] it is in this dazzling darkness that the divine things are given to the saints.

Thus the perfect contemplation of God and divine things is not simply an abstraction; but beyond this abstraction, there is a participation in divine things, a gift and a possession rather than just a process of negation. But these possessions and gifts are ineffable: If one speaks of them, one must have recourse to images and analogies—not because that is the way in which these things are seen, but because one cannot adumbrate what one has seen in any other way. Those, therefore, who do not listen in a reverent spirit to what is said about these ineffable things, which are necessarily expressed through images, regard the knowledge that is beyond wisdom as foolishness; trampling under foot the intelligible pearls,[27] they strive also to destroy as far as possible by their disputations those who have shown them to them.

19

As I have said, it is because of their love of men that the saints speak, so far as this is possible, about things ineffable, rejecting the error of those who in their ignorance imagine that, after the abstraction from beings, there remains only an absolute inaction, not an inaction surpassing all action. But, I repeat, these things remain ineffable by their very nature. This is why the great Denys says that after the abstraction from beings, there is no word but "an absence of words";[28] he also says, "After every elevation, we will be united with the Inexpressible."[29] But, despite this inexpressible character, negation alone does not suffice to enable the intellect to attain to superintelligible things. The ascent by negation is in fact only an apprehension of how all things are distinct from God;[30] it conveys only an image of the formless contemplation and of the fulfillment of the mind in contemplation, not being itself that fulfillment.

But those who, in the manner of angels, have been united to that light celebrate it by using the image of this total abstraction. The mystical union with the light teaches them that this light is superessentially transcendent to all things. Moreover, those judged worthy to receive the mystery with a faithful and prudent ear can also celebrate the divine and inconceivable light by means of an abstraction from all things. But they can only unite themselves to it and see if they have purified themselves by fulfillment of the commandments[31] and by consecrating their mind to pure and immaterial prayer, so as to receive the supernatural power of contemplation.

20

What then shall we call this power which is an activity neither of the senses nor of the intellect? How else except by using the expression of Solomon, who was wiser than all who preceded him: "a sensation intellectual and divine".[32] By adding those two adjectives, he urges his hearer to consider it neither as a sensation nor as an intellection, for neither is the activity of the intelligence a sensation, nor that of the senses an intellection. The "intellectual sensation" is thus different from both. Following the great Denys, one should perhaps call it union, and not knowledge. "One should realise," he says, "that our mind possesses both an intellectual power which permits it to see intelligible things, and also a capacity for that union which surpasses the nature of the intellect and allies it to that which transcends it."[33] And again: "The intellectual faculties become superfluous, like the senses, when the soul becomes deiform, abandoning itself to the rays of the inaccessible light in an unknown union by blind advances."[34] In this union, as St. Maximus puts it, "the saints by beholding the light of the hidden and more than ineffable glory themselves become capable of receiving blessed purity, together with the celestial powers".[35]

Let no one think that these great men are referring here to the ascent through the negative way. For the latter lies within the powers of whoever desires it; and it does not transform the soul so as to bestow on it the angelic dignity. While it liberates the understanding from other beings, it cannot by itself effect union with transcendent things. But purity of the passionate part of the soul effectively liberates the mind from all things through impassibility, and unites it through prayer to the grace of the Spirit; and through this grace the mind comes to enjoy the divine effulgence, and acquires an angelic and godlike form.

21

This is why the Fathers, following the great Denys, have called this state "spiritual sensation",[36] a phrase appropriate to, and somehow more expressive of, that mystical and ineffable contemplation. For at such a time man truly sees neither by the intellect nor by the body, but by the Spirit, and he knows that he sees supernaturally a light which surpasses light. But at that moment he does not know by what organ he sees this light, nor can he search out its nature, for the Spirit through whom he sees is untraceable. This was what Paul said when he heard ineffable words and saw invisible things: "I know not whether I saw out of the body or in the body."[37] In other words, he did not know whether it was his intellect or his body which saw.

Such a one does not see by sense perception, but his vision is as clear as or clearer than that by which the sight clearly perceives sensibilia. He sees by going out of himself,[38] for through the mysterious sweetness of his vision he is ravished beyond all objects and all objective thought, and even beyond himself.

Under the effect of the ecstasy, he forgets even prayer to God. It is this of which St. Isaac speaks, confirming the great and divine Gregory: "Prayer is the purity of the intellect which is produced with dread only from the light of the Holy Trinity."[39] And again, "Purity of spiritual mind is what allows the light of the Holy Trinity to shine forth at the time of prayer. . . . The mind then transcends prayer, and this state should not properly be called prayer, but a fruit of the pure prayer sent by the Holy Spirit. The mind does not pray a definite prayer, but finds itself in ecstasy in the midst of incomprehensible realities. It is indeed an ignorance superior to knowledge."[40]

This most joyful reality, which ravished Paul, and made his mind go out from every creature but yet return entirely to himself—this he beheld as a light of revelation, though not of sensible bodies; a light without limit, depth, height or lateral extension. He saw absolutely no limit to his vision and to the light which shone round about him; but rather it was as it were a sun infinitely brighter and greater than the universe, with himself standing in the midst of it, having become all eye.[41] Such, more or less, was his vision.

22

This is why the great Macarius says that this light is infinite and supercelestial.[42] Another saint, one of the most perfect, saw the whole universe contained in a single ray of this intelligible sun—even though he himself did not see this light as it is in itself, in its full extent, but only to that extent that he was capable of receiving it.[43] By this contemplation and by his supra-intelligible union with this light, he did not learn what it is by nature, but he learnt that it really exists, is supernatural and superessential, different from all things; that its being is absolute and unique, and that it mysteriously comprehends all in itself. This vision of the Infinite cannot permanently belong to any individual or to all men.[44]

He who does not see understands that he is himself incapable of vision because not perfectly conformed to the Spirit by a total purification, and not because of any limitation in the Object of vision. But when the vision comes to him, the recipient knows well that it *is* that light, even though he sees but dimly; he knows this from the impassible joy akin to the vision which he experiences, from the peace which fills his mind, and the fire of love for God which burns in him. The vision is granted him in proportion to his practice of what is pleasing to God, his avoidance of all that is not, his assiduity in prayer, and the longing of his entire soul for God; always he is being borne on to further progress[45] and experiencing even more resplendent contemplation. He understands then that his vision is infinite because it *is* a vision of the Infinite, and because he does not see the limit of that brilliance; but, all the more, he sees how feeble is his capacity to receive the light.

23

But he does not consider that the vision of which he has been deemed worthy *is* simply the Divine Nature. Just as the soul communicates life to the animated body—and we call this life "soul", while realising that the soul which is in us and which communicates life to the body is distinct from that life—so God, Who dwells in the God-bearing soul, communicates the light to it. However, the union of God the Cause of all with those worthy transcends that light. God, while remaining entirely in Himself, dwells entirely in us by His superessential power; and communicates to us not His nature, but His proper glory and splendour.[46]

The light is thus divine, and the saints rightly call it "divinity", because it is the source of deification. It is not only "divinity", but "deification-in-itself",[47] and thearchy. While it appears to produce a distinction and multiplication within the one God, yet it is nonetheless the Divine Principle, more-than-God, and more-than-Principle. The light is one in the one divinity, and therefore is itself the Divine Principle, more-than-God and more-than-Principle, since God is the ground of subsistence of divinity. Thus the doctors of the Church, following the great Areopagite Denys, call "divinity" the deifying gift that proceeds from God. So when Gaius asked Denys how God could be beyond the thearchy, he replied in his letter: "If you consider as 'divinity' the reality of the deifying gift which divinises us, and if this Gift is the principle of divinisation, then He Who is above all principle is also above what you thus call 'divinity'."[48] So the Fathers tell us that the divine grace of the suprasensible light is God. But God in his nature does not simply identify Himself with this grace, because He is able not only to illumine and deify the mind, but also to bring forth from nonbeing every intellectual essence.

C.   The Hesychast method of prayer, and the transformation of the body

I. ii. 1

My brother, do you not hear the words of the Apostle, "Our bodies are the temple of the Holy Spirit which is in us,"[1] and again, "We are the house of God"?[2] For God Himself says, "I will dwell in them and will walk in them and I shall be their God."[3] So why should anyone who possesses mind grow indignant at the thought that our mind dwells in that whose nature it is to become the dwelling place of God? How can it be that God at the beginning caused the mind to inhabit the body? Did even He do ill? Rather, brother, such views befit the heretics, who claim that the body is an evil thing, a fabrication of the Wicked One.[4]

As for us, we think the mind becomes evil through dwelling on fleshly thoughts, but that there is nothing bad in the body, since the body is not evil in itself.[5] . . . If the Apostle calls the body "death" (saying, "Who will deliver me from the body of this death?"[6]), this is because the material and corporeal thought does really have the form of the body. Then, comparing it to spiritual and divine ideas, he justly calls it "body"—yet not simply "body" but "body of death". Further on, he makes it even clearer that what he is attacking is not the body, but the sinful desire that entered in because of the Fall: "I am sold to sin,"[7] he says. But he who is sold is not a slave by nature. And again: "I well know that what is good does not dwell in me, that is, in the flesh."[8] You note that he does not say the flesh is evil, but what inhabits it. Likewise, there is nothing evil in the fact that the mind indwells

41

the body; what is evil is "the law which is in our members, which fights against the law of the mind".[9]

2

This is why we set ourselves against this "law of sin",[10] and drive it out of the body, installing in its place the oversight of the mind, and in this way establishing a law appropriate for each power of the soul, and for every member of the body. For the senses we ordain the object and limit of their scope, this work of the law being called "temperance". In the affective part of the soul, we bring about the best state, which bears the name "love". And we improve the rational part by rejecting all that impedes the mind from elevating itself towards God (this part of the law we call "watchfulness").[11] He who has purified his body by temperance, who by divine love has made an occasion of virtue from his wishes and desires,[12] who has presented to God a mind purified by prayer, acquires and sees in himself the grace promised to those whose hearts have been purified. He can then say with Paul: "God, who has ordered light to shine from darkness, has made His light to shine in our hearts, in order that we may be enlightened by the knowledge of the glory of God, in the face of Jesus Christ";[13] but he adds, "We carry this treasure in earthen vessels."[14] So we carry the Father's light in the face[15] of Jesus Christ in earthen vessels, that is, in our bodies, in order to know the glory of the Holy Spirit. Shall we be treating the greatness of the mind unworthily if we guard our own mind within the body?[16] What man (I do not say spiritual man) endowed with human intelligence would say that, even if bereft of divine grace?

3

Our soul is a unique reality, yet possessing multiple powers. It uses as an instrument the body, which by nature co-exists with it. But as for that power of the soul we call mind,[17] what instruments does that use in its operations? No one has ever supposed that the mind has its seat in the nails or the eyelids, the nostrils or the lips. Everyone is agreed in locating it within us, but there are differences of opinion as to which inner organ serves the mind as primary instrument. Some[18] place the mind in the brain, as in a kind of acropolis; others[19] hold that its vehicle is the very centre of the heart, and that element therein which is purified of the breath of animal soul.[20]

We ourselves know exactly that our rational part is not confined within us as in a container, for it is incorporeal, nor is it outside of us, for it is conjoined to us; but it is in the heart, as in an instrument. We did not learn this from any man, but from Him who moulded man, who showed that "it is not what goes into a man that defiles a man, but what goes out by the mouth",[21] adding "for it is from the heart that evil thoughts come".[22] And the great Macarius says also, "The heart directs the entire organism, and when grace gains possession of the heart, it reigns over all the thoughts and all the members; for it is there, in the heart, that the mind and all the thoughts of the soul have their seat."[23]

Thus our heart [24] is the place of the rational faculty, the first rational organ of the body. Consequently, when we seek to keep watch over and correct our reason by a rigorous sobriety, with what are we to keep watch, if we do not gather together[25] our mind, which has been dissipated abroad by the senses, and lead it back again into the interior, to the selfsame heart which is the seat of the thoughts? This is why the justly named[26] Macarius immediately goes on to say, "It is there one must look to see if grace has inscribed the laws of the Spirit."[27] Where but in the heart, the controlling organ, the throne of grace, where the mind and all the thoughts of the soul are to be found?

Can you not see, then, how essential it is that those who have determined to pay attention to themselves in inner quiet should gather together the mind and enclose it in the body, and especially in that "body" most interior to the body, which we call the heart?

4

For if, as the Psalmist says, "all the glory of the king's daughter is within",[28] why do we search for it without? And if, according to the Apostle, "God has given His Spirit to cry in our hearts, Abba, Father,"[29] how is it we too do not pray with the Spirit in our hearts? If, as the Lord of the prophets and apostles teaches, "the Kingdom of God is within us",[30] does it not follow that a man will be excluded from the Kingdom if he devotes his energies to making his mind go out from within himself? For the "upright heart", Solomon says, "seeks that sense"[31] which he elsewhere calls "spiritual and divine",[32] which the Fathers urge us all to acquire, saying, "The spiritual mind seeks ever to acquire[33] a spiritual sense; let us not cease to seek that sense since it is in us, yet not in us."[34]

Do you not see that if one desires to combat sin and acquire vir-

tue, to find the reward of the struggle for virtue, or rather the intellectual sense, earnest[35] of that reward, one must force the mind to
return within the body and oneself? On the other hand, to make the
mind "go out", not only from fleshly thoughts, but out of the body
itself,[36] with the aim of contemplating intelligible visions—that is the
greatest of the Hellenic errors, the root and source of all heresies, an
invention of demons, a doctrine which engenders folly and is itself
the product of madness. This is why those who speak by demonic in-
spiration become beside themselves, not knowing what they are saying.[37] As for us, we recollect the mind not only within the body and
heart, but also within itself.

5

There are, however, those who assert that the mind is not separate from the soul but is interior to it, and who therefore question
how it can be recalled within. It would seem such people are unaware
that the essence of the mind is one thing, its energy another. Or rather, they are well aware of this, and prefer to range themselves with
the deceitful, and prevaricate over an ambiguity. "For such men,
sharpened to controversy by dialectic, do not accept the simplicity of
the spiritual doctrine", as the great Basil says. "They pervert the
force of truth by the antitheses of false knowledge,[38] aided by the persuasive arguments of sophistry."[39] Such indeed are those who, without being spiritual themselves, consider themselves fit to decide and
teach spiritual matters!

Has it not occurred to them that the mind is like the eye, which
sees other visible objects but cannot see itself?[40] The mind operates in
part according to its function of external observation: This is what
the great Denys calls the movement of the mind "along a straight
line";[41] and on the other hand, it returns upon itself, when it beholds
itself; this movement the same Father calls "circular".[42] This last is
the most excellent and most appropriate activity of the mind, by
which it comes to transcend itself and be united to God. "For the
mind", says St. Basil, "which is not dispersed abroad" (notice how he
says "dispersed"? What is dispersed, then, needs to be recollected),
"returns to itself, and through itself mounts towards God"[43] as by an
infallible road. Denys, that unerring contemplator of intelligible
things, says also that this movement of the mind cannot succumb to
any error.[44]

GREGORY PALAMAS

6

The Father of Lies is always desiring to lead man towards those errors which he himself promotes; but up to now (as far as we know) he has found no collaborator who has tried to lead others to this goal by good words. But today, if what you tell me is true, it seems he has found accomplices who have even composed treatises towards this end, and who seek to persuade men (even those who have embraced the higher life of hesychasm) that it would be better for them to keep the mind *outside* of the body during prayer.[45] They do not even respect the clear and authoritative words of John, who writes in his *Ladder of Divine Ascent*, "The hesychast is one who seeks to circumscribe the incorporeal in his body."[46]

This is exactly the tradition, and our spiritual Fathers have also handed it down to us, and rightly so. For if the hesychast does not circumscribe the mind in his body, how can he make to enter himself the One who has clothed himself in the body, and Who thus penetrates all organised matter, insofar as He is its natural form?[47] For the external aspect and divisibility of matter is not compatible with the essence of the mind, unless matter itself truly begins to live, having acquired a form of life conformable to the union with Christ.[48]

7

You see, brother, how John [49] teaches us that it is enough to examine the matter in a human (let alone a spiritual) manner, to see that it is absolutely necessary to recall or keep the mind within the body, when one determines to be truly in possession of oneself and to be a monk worthy of the name, according to the inner man.

On the other hand, it is not out of place to teach people, especially beginners, that they should look at themselves, and introduce their own mind within themselves through control of breathing.[50] A prudent man will not forbid someone who does not as yet contemplate himself to use certain methods to recall his mind within himself, for those newly approaching this struggle find that their mind, when recollected, continually becomes dispersed again. It is thus necessary for such people constantly to bring it back once more; but in their inexperience, they fail to grasp that nothing in the world is in fact more difficult to contemplate and more mobile and shifting than the mind.[51]

This is why certain masters recommend them to control the movement inwards and outwards of the breath, and to hold it back a little;[52] in this way, they will also be able to control the mind together with the breath—this, at any rate, until such time as they have made progress, with the aid of God, have restrained the intellect from becoming distracted by what surrounds it, have purified it and truly become capable of leading it to a "unified recollection".[53] One can state that this recollection is a spontaneous effect of the attention of the mind, for the to-and-fro movement of the breath becomes quietened during intensive reflection, especially with those who maintain inner quiet[54] in body and soul.

Such men, in effect, practise a spiritual Sabbath, and, as far as is possible, cease from all personal activity. They strip the cognitive powers of the soul of every changing, mobile and diversified operation, of all sense perceptions and, in general, of all corporal activity that is under our control; as to acts which are not entirely under our control, like breathing, these they restrain as far as possible.

8

In the case of those who have made progress in hesychasm, all this comes to pass without painful effort and without their worrying about it, for the perfect entry of the soul within itself spontaneously produces such inner detachment. But with beginners none of these things comes about without toil;[55] for patience is a fruit of love, "for love bears all",[56] and teaches us to practise patience with all our strength in order to attain love; and this is a case in point.

But why delay over these matters? Everyone who has the experience can only laugh at the contradictions of the inexperienced; for they have learnt not through words but effort, and the experience which indicates the pains they take. It is effort which brings the useful fruits, and challenges the sterile views of the lovers of disputation and ostentation.

One of the great masters teaches, "After the transgression, the inner man naturally is conformed to external forms."[57] Thus, the man who seeks to make his mind return to itself needs to propel it not only in a straight line but also in the circular motion that is infallible.[58] How should such a one not gain great profit if, instead of letting his eye roam hither and thither, he should fix it on his breast or on his navel, as a point of concentration?[59] For in this way, he will not only gather himself together externally, conforming as far as possible to the inner movement he seeks for his mind; he will also, by disposing his body in such a position, recall into the interior of the heart a power which is ever flowing outwards through the faculty of sight. And if the power of the intelligible animal is situated at the centre of the belly,[60] since there the law of sin exercises its rule and gives it sustenance, why should we not place there "the law of the mind which combats"[61] this power, duly armed with prayer, so that the evil spirit who has been driven away thanks to the "bath of regeneration"[62] may not return to install himself there with seven other spirits even more evil, so that "the latter state becomes worse than the first"?[63]

9

"Pay attention to yourself", says Moses,[64] meaning, to the whole of yourself, not just a part. How? By the mind, evidently, for by no other instrument is it possible to be attentive to the whole of oneself. Place therefore this guard over your soul and body: It will easily deliver you from the evil passions of the body and soul. Maintain this watch, this attention, this self-control, or rather mount guard, be vigilant, keep watch! For it is thus that you will make the disobedient flesh subject to the Spirit, and "there will no longer be a hidden word in your heart".[65] "If the spirit of him who dominates"—that is to say, of the evil spirits and passions—"lifts himself up over you," says Scripture, "on no account shift your ground";[66] in other words, never leave any part of your soul or any member of your body without surveillance.

In this way, you will become unapproachable to the spirits that attack you from below, and you will be able to present yourself with boldness to "Him who searches the reins and the heart";[67] and that indeed without His scrutinising you, for you will have scrutinised yourself. Paul tells us, "If we judge ourselves, we will not be judged."[68] You will then have the blessed experience of David and you will address yourself to God, saying, "The shadows are no longer darkness thanks to you, and the night will be for me as clear as the day, for it is you who have taken possession of my reins."[69] David says in effect, "Not only have you made the passionate part of my soul entirely yours, but if there is a spark of desire in my body, it has returned to its source, and has thereby become elevated and united to you."[70]

For just as those who abandon themselves to sensual and corruptible pleasures fix all the desires of their soul upon the flesh, and indeed become entirely "flesh", so that (as Scripture says) "the Spirit of God cannot dwell in them",[71] so too, in the case of those who have elevated their minds to God and exalted their souls with divine longing, their flesh also is being transformed and elevated, participating together with the soul in the divine communion, and becoming itself a dwelling and possession of God; for it is no longer the seat of enmity towards God, and no longer possesses desires contrary to the Spirit.

II. ii. 5.

When we return to interior reflection, it is necessary to calm the sensations aroused by external activities. But why should one calm those provoked by the dispositions of the soul, the good dispositions? Is there a method of ridding oneself of them, once one has returned into oneself? And indeed, for what reason should one seek to dispose of them, since they in no way impede one, but rather contribute to the greatest possible extent to our integration?[72]

For this body which is united to us has been attached to us as a fellow-worker by God, or rather placed under our control. Thus we will repress it, if it is in revolt, and accept it, if it conducts itself as it should. The hearing and sight are more pure and more easily conformed to reason than the touch, but nonetheless one will pay them no attention, nor be disturbed by them in any way, except when what we see or hear affects us disagreeably.

It is the body in particular which suffers as regards sensation, especially when we fast and do not provide it with nourishment from without. For this reason, people recollected within themselves and detached from external things, insofar as they remain undistracted, maintain in a state of inaction those senses which do not operate without external stimulus. As to those sensations which continue active even in the absence of external objects, how should they be disposed to inactivity, especially when they tend towards the end that is prescribed for them? For as all who have experienced ascetical combat, sensation painful to the touch[73] is of greatest benefit to those who practise inner prayer. They have no need here of words, for they know by experience, and do not agree with those who seek such things merely in a theoretical way, for they regard this as "the knowledge that puffs up".[74]

GREGORY PALAMAS

6

In every case, those who practise true mental prayer must liberate themselves from the passions, and reject any contact with objects which obstruct it, for in this way they are able to acquire undisrupted and pure prayer. As for those not yet arrived at this degree, but who seek to attain it, they must gain the mastery over every sensual pleasure, completely rejecting the passions, for the body's capacity to sin must be mortified; that is, one must be released from domination by the passionate emotions. Similarly the judgement must vanquish the evil passions which move in the world of mind, that is, it must rise above the sensual delights.

For it is the case that if we cannot taste mental prayer, not even as it were with the slightest touch of our lips, and if we are dominated by passionate emotions, then we certainly stand in need of the physical suffering that comes from fasting, vigils and similar things, if we are to apply ourselves to prayer.[75] This suffering alone mortifies the body's inclination to sin, and moderates and weakens the thoughts that provoke violent passions. Moreover, it is this which brings about within us the start of holy compunction,[76] through which both the stain of past faults is done away and the divine favour especially attracted, and which disposes one towards prayer. For "God will not despise a bruised heart", as David says;[77] and according to Gregory the Theologian, "God heals in no more certain way than through suffering."[78] This is why the Lord taught us in the Gospels that prayer can do great things when combined with fasting.[79]

7

To become "insensible"[80] is in effect to do away with prayer; the Fathers call this "petrifaction".[81] Was not this man Barlaam the first to . . . criticise those who have real knowledge because they feel physical pain? Indeed, certain of the Fathers have declared that fasting is of the essence of prayer: "Hunger is the stuff of prayer", they say.[82] Others say it is its "quality", for they know that prayer without compunction has no quality.

And what will you reply when you are told, "Thirst and vigils oppressed the heart; and when the heart was oppressed, tears flowed"?[83] And again: "Prayer is the mother of tears, and also their daughter."[84] Do you see that this physical distress not only causes no obstacle to prayer, but contributes largely to it?[85] And what are those tears whose mother and daughter is prayer? Are they not by nature wretched, bitter and wounding for those who have scarcely tasted "the blessed affliction", but become sweet and inoffensive for those who have the fulness of joy? How is it that prayer does not dispel the bodily motions which produce a sensible joy and pain, or rather, how do these motions engender prayer and are engendered by it? Why does God bestow them as a grace, according to him who says: "If in your prayer, you have obtained tears, then God has touched the eyes of your heart, and you have recovered intellectual sight"?[86]

8

Paul was "ravished to the third heaven, and did not know whether he was in the body or out of the body"[87] for he had forgotten all that concerns the body. So, our opponents ask, if someone who strives towards God in prayer has to cease from the perception of corporeal things, how can such things be gifts of God, if he who so strives has to reject them? But it is not only bodily activities which ought to be abandoned by one who strives towards the divine union, but also intellectual ones: "All the divine lights, and every elevation towards all the holy summits must be left behind", as the great Denys says.[88] . . . "And how can these things come from grace," asks Barlaam, "when one does not perceive them during the mental prayer that unites man to God? They serve no purpose, whereas all that comes from Him is to some purpose." . . . But do you suppose the divine union surpasses only useless things, and not also things great and necessary? It is obvious that you yourself never elevate yourself above useless things: otherwise, you would realise that union with God surpasses even things that are useful in themselves.

9

. . . This spiritual grace in the heart, alas, you call "fantasy of the imagination, presenting to us a deceptive likeness of the heart".[89] However, those judged worthy of this grace know that it is not a fantasy produced by the imagination, and that it does not originate with us, nor appear only to disappear; but rather, it is a permanent energy produced by grace, united to the soul and rooted in it, a fountain of holy joy that attracts the soul to itself, liberating it from multiform and material images and making it joyfully despise every fleshly thing. (I call "fleshly thing" that which in our thoughts derives from the pleasures of the body, which attaches itself to our thoughts, appearing as something agreeable to them and dragging them downwards.)

As to that which takes place in the body, yet derives from a soul full of spiritual joy, it is a spiritual reality, even though it does work itself out in the body. When the pleasure originating from the body enters the mind, it conveys to the latter a corporeal aspect, without the body's being itself in any way improved by this communion with a superior reality, but rather giving an inferior quality to the mind, and this is why the whole man is called "flesh", as was said of those overwhelmed by the divine wrath: "My Spirit will not dwell in these men, because they are flesh."[90] Conversely, the spiritual joy which comes from the mind into the body is in no way corrupted by the communion with the body, but transforms the body and makes it spiritual, because it then rejects all the evil appetites of the body; it no longer drags the soul downwards, but is elevated together with it.[91] Thus it is that the whole man becomes spirit, as it is written: "He who is born of Spirit, is spirit."[92] All these things, indeed, become clear by experience.

12

Our philosopher brings the further objection: That to love those activities which are common to the passionate part of the soul and to the body serves to nail the soul to the body, and to fill the soul with darkness.

But what pain or pleasure or movement is not a common activity of both body and soul? ... There are indeed blessed passions and common activities of body and soul, which, far from nailing the spirit to the flesh, serve to draw the flesh to a dignity close to that of the spirit, and persuade it too to tend towards what is above. Such spiritual activities, as we said above, do not enter the mind from the body, but descend into the body from the mind, in order to transform the body into something better and to deify it by these actions and passions.

For just as the divinity of the Word of God incarnate is common to soul and body, since He has deified the flesh through the mediation of the soul to make it also accomplish the works of God; so similarly, in spiritual man, the grace of the Spirit, transmitted to the body through the soul, grants to the body also the experience of things divine, and allows it the same blessed experiences as the soul undergoes.

The soul, since it experiences divine things,[93] doubtless possesses a passionate part, praiseworthy and divine: or rather, there is within us a single passionate aspect which is capable of thus becoming praiseworthy and divine.[94]

When the soul pursues this blessed activity, it deifies the body also; which, being no longer driven by corporeal and material passions—although those who lack experience of this think that it is always so driven—returns to itself and rejects all contact with evil things. Indeed, it inspires its own sanctification and inalienable divinisation, as the miracle-working relics of the saints clearly demonstrate.

What of Stephen, the first martyr, whose face, even while he was yet living, shone like the face of an angel?[95] Did not his body also experience divine things? Is not such an experience and the activity allied to it common to soul and body? Far from nailing the soul to terrestrial and corporeal thoughts and filling it with darkness, as the philosopher alleges, such a common experience constitutes an ineffable bond and union with God. It elevates the body itself in a marvellous way, and sets it far apart from evil and earthly passions. For as the Prophet says, "Those whom God has filled with power have been lifted far above the earth."[96]

Such are the realities or mysterious energies brought about in the bodies of those who during their entire life have devoutly embraced holy hesychasm; that which seems to be contrary to reason in them is in fact superior to reason. These things escape and transcend the intellect of one who seeks merely in a theoretical way, and not knowledge of them by practice and the experience that comes through it. Such a man impiously lays hands on the sacred and wickedly rends apart the holy, for he does not approach these things with that faith which alone can attain to the truth that lies above reason.[97]

13

. . . Indeed every man of sense knows well that most of the charisms of the Spirit are granted to those worthy of them at the time of prayer. "Ask and it shall be given",[98] the Lord says. This applies not only to being ravished "even to the third heaven",[99] but to all the gifts of the Spirit. The gift of diversity of tongues[100] and their interpretation, which Paul recommends us to acquire by prayer, shows that certain charisms operate through the body. . . . The same is true of the word of instruction,[101] the gift of healing,[102] the performing of miracles,[103] and Paul's laying-on of hands by which he communicated the Holy Spirit.[104]

In the case of the gifts of instruction and of tongues and their interpretation, even though these are acquired by prayer, yet it is possible that they may operate even when prayer is absent from the soul. But healings and miracles never take place unless the soul of the one exercising either gift be in a state of intense mental prayer and his body in perfect tune with his soul.

In short, the transmission of the Spirit is effected not only when prayer is present in the soul, a prayer which mystically accomplishes the union with the perpetual source of these benefits; not only when one is practising mental prayer, since it is not recorded that the apostles uttered any audible words at the moment of laying on their hands.[105] This communication takes place, then, not only during the mental prayer of the soul, but also at those moments when the body is operating, when for instance the hands through which the Holy Spirit is sent down are touching the man who is being ordained. How can you say that such charisms involving the body are not just as much gifts of God, given for the good of those who pray to possess them, alleging as your reason that those "ravished to the third heaven" must forget what concerns the body?

14

... Although God makes those who pray sincerely go out of themselves, rendering them transcendent to their natures and mysteriously ravished away to heaven, yet even in such cases, since they are concentrated within themselves, it is through the mediation of their souls and body that God effects things supernatural, mysterious and incomprehensible to the wise of this world.[106]

When the Holy Spirit visited the apostles in the Temple,[107] where "they were persevering in prayer and supplication",[108] He did not give them ecstasy, did not ravish them to heaven, but endowed them with tongues of fire, making them pronounce *words*[109]—which, according to you, those in ecstasy should forget, since they must be forgetful of themselves. Again, when Moses was silent, God said to him, "Why do you cry to me?"[110] This reference to his voice shows that he was in prayer; but since he prayed while remaining silent, he was clearly engaged in mental prayer. Did he then abandon his senses, not noticing the people, their cries, and the danger hanging over them, nor the staff that was in his visible hand? Why did not

God ravish him at that moment, why did He not deliver him from the senses (which you seem to think the sole gift of God to those who pray); but directed his attention towards his visible staff, conferring great power not only on his soul but also on his body and arm— things which according to you, those praying mentally ought to forget? Why, while remaining silent, did he strike the sea with his staff which he was holding in his hand, first to divide the sea, and later, after the crossing, to close it? Had he not in his soul the constant memory of God, was he not sublimely united by mental prayer to Him Who alone could accomplish such things through him?[111] Yet, at the same time, he was engaging in these activities through the body in a sensible manner.

19

... Impassibility does not consist in mortifying the passionate part of the soul, but in removing it from evil to good, and directing its energies towards divine things ... and the impassible man is one who no longer possesses any evil dispositions, but is rich in good ones, who is marked by the virtues, as men of passion are marked by evil pleasures; who has tamed his irascible and concupiscent appetites (which constitute the passionate part of the soul), to the faculties of knowledge, judgement and reason in the soul, just as men of passion subject their reason to the passions.[112] For it is the *misuse* of the powers of the soul which engenders the terrible passions, just as misuse of the knowledge of created things engenders the "wisdom which has become folly".[113]

But if one uses these things properly, then through the knowledge of created things, spiritually understood, one will arrive at knowledge of God; and through the passionate part of the soul which has been orientated towards the end for which God created it, one will practise the corresponding virtues: with the concupiscent appetite, one will embrace charity, and with the irascible, one will practise patience. It is thus not the man who has killed the passionate part of his soul who has the preeminence, for such a one would have no momentum or activity to acquire a divine state and right dispositions and relationship with God;[114] but rather, the prize goes to him who has put that part of his soul under subjection, so that by its obedience to the mind, which is by nature appointed to rule, it may ever tend towards God, as is right, by the uninterrupted remembrance[115] of Him. Thanks to this remembrance, he will come to possess a divine disposition, and cause the soul to progress towards the highest state of all, the love of God. Through this love, he will accomplish the commandments of Him whom he loves, in accord with Scripture, and will put into practise and acquire a pure and perfect love for his neighbour,[116] something that cannot exist without impassibility.

20

Such is the way which leads through impassibility to perfect love, an excellent way which takes us to the heights.[117] It is most appropriate for those detached from the world, for they are consecrated to God, and this union allows them continually to converse with Him with a pure mind. They easily reject the refuse of the evil passions, and preserve for themselves the treasure of love.

As to those who live in the world, they must force themselves to use the things of this world in conformity with the commandments of God. Will not the passionate part of the soul, as a result of this violence,[118] be also brought to act according to the commandments? Such forcing, by dint of habituation, makes easy our acceptance of God's commandments, and transforms our changeable disposition into a fixed state. This condition brings about a steady hatred towards evil states and dispositions of soul; and hatred of evil duly produces the impassibility which in turn engenders love for the unique Good. Thus one must offer to God the passionate part of the soul, alive and active, that it may be a living sacrifice. As the Apostle said of our bodies, "I exhort you, by the mercy of God, to offer your bodies as a living sacrifice, holy, acceptable to God."[119] How can this be done?

Our eyes must acquire a gentle glance, attractive to others, and conveying the mercy from on high (for it is written, "He who has a gentle look will receive grace").[120] Similarly, our ears must be attentive to the divine instructions, not only to hear them, but (as David says) "to remember the commandments of God . . . in order to perform them",[121] not becoming "a forgetful hearer, but fixing the gaze on the perfect law of liberty, pressing onwards, and acquiring blessedness in the accomplishment", as the apostolic brother of God teaches.[122] Our tongues, our hands and feet must likewise be at the service of the Divine Will. Is not such a practice of the commandments of God a common activity of body and soul, and how can such activity darken and blind the soul?

D. Deification in Christ

II. iii: 8

... The monks know that the essence of God transcends the fact of being inaccessible to the senses, since God is not only above all created things, but is even beyond Godhead. The excellence of Him Who surpasses all things is not only beyond all affirmation, but also beyond all negation;[1] it exceeds all excellence that is attainable by the mind. This hypostatic[2] light, seen spiritually[3] by the saints, they know by experience to exist, as they tell us, and to exist not symbolically only, as do manifestations produced by fortuitous events; but it is an illumination immaterial and divine, a grace invisibly seen and ignorantly known.[4] *What* it is, they do not pretend to know.[5]

9

... This light is not the essence of God, for that is inaccessible and incommunicable;[6] it is not an angel, for it bears the marks of the Master. Sometimes it makes a man go out from the body or else, without separating him from the body, it elevates him to an ineffable height. At other times, it transforms the body, and communicates its own splendour to it when, miraculously, the light which deifies the body becomes accessible to the bodily eyes.[7] Thus indeed did the great Arsenius appear when engaged in hesychastic combat;[8] similarly Stephen, whilst being stoned,[9] and Moses, when he descended from the mountain.[10] Sometimes the light "speaks" clearly, as it were with ineffable words, to him who contemplates it. Such was the case with Paul.[11] According to Gregory the Theologian, "It descends from the elevated places where it dwells, so that He who in His own

57

nature from eternity is neither visible to nor containable by any being may in a certain measure be contained by a created nature."[12] He who has received this light, by concentrating upon himself, constantly perceives in his mind that same reality which the children of the Jews called *manna*, the bread that came down from on high. . . .[13]

10

. . . The hesychasts in fact never claim that this light is an angel. Having been initiated by the teaching of the Fathers, they know that the vision of angels takes place in various ways, according to the capacities of those who behold it: sometimes in the form of a concrete essence, accessible to the senses, and visible even to creatures full of passions and totally foreign to all initiation; sometimes under the form of an ethereal essence which the soul itself can only see in part; sometimes as a true vision, which only those who are purified and who see spiritually are worthy to behold. But you,[14] who have not been initiated into these different modes of seeing angels, think to show that the angels are invisible to one another not because they are incorporeal, but in their essence; and implicitly you class the contemplators of God with Balaam's ass, which also is said to have seen an angel![15]

11

Elsewhere you claim that the mind contemplates God "not in some other hypostasis; but when purified at once of passions and ignorance, in beholding itself, it sees God in itself, since it is made in His image."[16] You also believe that those who claim to see in this way the very essence of the mind under the form of light are in accord with the most mystical Christian tradition. But hesychasts know that the purified and illuminated mind, when clearly participating in the grace of God, also beholds other mystical and supernatural visions— for in seeing itself, it sees more than itself: It does not simply contemplate some other object, or simply its own image,[17] but rather the glory impressed on its own image by the grace of God. This radiance reinforces the mind's power to transcend itself, and accomplish that union with those better things which is beyond understanding. By this union, the mind sees God in the Spirit in a manner transcending human powers.

. . . You claim that the mind can see God only when purified not only of the passions but of ignorance as well:[18] yet the saints make no mention of the latter. They purify themselves of evil passions and transcend all knowledge by uninterrupted and immaterial prayer, and it is then that they begin to see God. . . . For they never cease to keep watch over themselves, not wasting time to find out if someone else—a Scythian perhaps, a Persian, or an Egyptian—claims such-and-such knowledge, nor bothering about this "purification from ignorance". They know perfectly well that ignorance of that kind in no way hinders the vision of God.

For if the fulfillment of the commandments has no other result than the purification of the passions; and if, according to God's promise, only this keeping of the commandments will procure the presence, the indwelling and manifestation of God, is it not a flagrant error to speak in addition about this further purification from ignorance . . . a "purification" which, as we have shown, in fact causes knowledge to vanish?

12

. . . Barlaam first spells out the reasons which, he claims, led the monks whom he is accusing to believe the essence of God (or its emanation) to be a perceptible light.[19] It was, he says, because they saw in Scripture that most of the visions and revelations of which the saints were mystical beneficiaries occurred and appeared through and in a light. . . . But why should one consider the essence of God as a light of this kind? None of us has ever defined a contemplative as one who has seen the divine *essence!* So if the contemplative does not see the essence of God, and if according to you the hesychasts call "contemplative" one who sees a certain light, it is evident that they do not consider the light seen by such contemplatives to be the divine essence.

15

It is our purpose to communicate the teaching on the light of grace of those long-revered saints whose wisdom comes from experience, proclaiming that "such is the teaching of Scripture".[20] Thus we set forth as a summary the words of Isaac, the faithful interpreter of these things:[21] "Our soul", he affirms, "possesses two eyes, as all the Fathers tell us. . . . Yet the sight which is proper to each 'eye' is not for the same use: with one eye, we behold the secrets of nature, that is to say, the power of God, His wisdom and providence towards us, things comprehensible by virtue of the greatness of His governance. With the other eye, we contemplate the glory of His holy nature, since it pleases God to introduce us to the spiritual mysteries."[22]

Since then these are eyes, what they see is a light; but since each possesses a power of vision designed for a particular use, a certain duality appears in the contemplation of this light, since each eye sees a different light, invisible to the other eye. As the divine Isaac has explained, the one is the apprehension of the power, wisdom and providence of God, and in general, knowledge of the Creator through the creatures; the other is contemplation, not of the divine nature . . . but of the *glory* of His nature, which the Saviour has bestowed on His disciples, and through them, on all who believe in Him and have manifested their faith through their works. This glory He clearly desired them to see, for He says to the Father, "I will that they contemplate the glory You have given Me, for You have loved Me since the foundation of the world."[23] And again, "Glorify Me, Father, with that glory I have had from You since before the world began."[24]

Thus to our human nature He has given the glory of the Godhead, but not the divine nature; for the nature of God is one thing, His glory another, even though they be inseparable one from another. However, even though this glory is different from the divine nature, it cannot be classified amongst the things subject to time, for in its transcendence "it is not",[25] because it belongs to the divine nature in an ineffable manner.

Yet it is not only to that human composite which is united to His hypostasis[26] that He has given this glory which transcends all things, but also to His disciples. "Father," He says, "I have given them the glory which You gave Me, so that they may be perfectly one."[27] But He wishes also that they should see this glory,[28] which we possess in our inmost selves and through which properly speaking we see God.

16

How then do we possess and see this glory of the divine nature? Is it in examining the causes of things and seeking through them the knowledge of the power, wisdom and providence of God? But, as we have said, it is another eye of the soul which sees all this, which does not see the divine light, "the glory of his nature" (in St. Isaac's words). This light is thus different from the light synonymous with knowledge.[29]

Therefore, not every man who possesses the knowledge of created things, or who sees through the mediation of such knowledge has God dwelling in him; but he merely possesses knowledge of creatures, and from this by means of analogy he infers the existence of God. As to him who mysteriously possesses and sees this light, he knows and possesses God in himself, no longer by analogy, but by a true contemplation, transcendent to all creatures, for he is never separated from the eternal glory.

Let us not, then, turn aside incredulous before the superabundance of these blessings; but let us have faith in Him who has participated in our nature and granted it in return the glory of His own nature, and let us seek how to acquire this glory and see it. How? By keeping the divine commandments.[30] For the Lord has promised to manifest Himself to the man who keeps them, a manifestation He calls His own indwelling and that of the Father, saying, "If anyone loves Me, he will keep My word, and My Father will love him, and We will come to him and will make our abode with him",[31] and "I will manifest Myself to him."[32] And it is clear that in mentioning His "word", He means His commandments, since earlier He speaks of "commandments" in place of "word": "He who possesses and keeps My commandments, that is the man who loves Me."[33]

17

We have here a proof . . . that this contemplation of God is not a form of knowledge,[34] even though Barlaam's greatest desire is that the opposite should be true. For our own part, if we refuse to call this contemplation "knowledge", it is by reason of its transcendence—just as we also say that God is not being, for we believe Him to be above being. But how to show that this divine light is different from knowledge?

Our philosopher observes that "the observance of the commandments cannot remove the darkness of ignorance from the soul; that can be done only through learning and the perseverance in study that this entails."[35] But what does not even remove ignorance cannot give knowledge! Yet what according to him does not lead to knowledge, according to the Saviour's words, brings us to contemplation. Indeed, this contemplation is not knowledge, and not only should one not think or speak of it as such, but it is not in fact knowable (unless this term is employed in an improper and equivocal sense).[36] Rather, employing the word "knowable" in its strict sense, but giving it a transcendent meaning, one should believe it to be superior to all

61

knowledge, and to all contemplation which depends on knowledge, since nothing surpasses the indwelling and manifestation of God in us, nothing equals it, nothing approaches it.

But we also know that the fulfillment of the commandments of God gives true knowledge, since it is through this that the soul gains health. How could a rational soul be healthy, if it is sick in its cognitive faculty? So we know that the commandments of God also grant knowledge, and not that alone, but deification also. This we possess in a perfect manner, through the Spirit, seeing in ourselves the glory of God, when it pleases God to lead us to spiritual mysteries, in the manner indicated by St. Isaac.[37]

18

... But let us also hear what certain other saints who preceded him have to say of the glory of God, mysteriously and secretly visible to the initiated alone. Let us look first at the eyewitnesses and apostles of our one God and Father Jesus Christ, from Whom all paternity[38] in the fulness of Holy Church is derived.[39] And, first among them, let us listen to their leader Peter, who says, "It is not by following improbable fables that we have come to know the power and presence of Our Lord Jesus Christ, but because we have ourselves become witnesses of His greatness."[40] And here is another apostolic eyewitness of this glory: "Keeping themselves awake, Peter and his companions beheld the glory of Christ."[41] What glory? Another evangelist testifies: "His face shone like the sun, and His garments became white like the light",[42] showing them that He was Himself the God Who, in the Psalmist's words, "wraps himself in light as in a mantle".[43]

But, after having testified to his vision of Christ's glory on the holy mountain[44]—of a light which illumines, strange though it may be, the ears themselves (for they contemplated also a luminous cloud from which words reverberated)—Peter goes on to say, "This confirms the prophetic word."[45] What is this prophetic word which the vision of light confirms for you, O contemplators of God? What if not that verse that God "wraps Himself in light as in a mantle"? He continues, "You would do well to pay attention to that prophetic word, as to a lamp which shines in a dark place till the day dawns."[46] What day, if not that which dawned in Thabor? "Let the morning star arise!"[47] What star, if not that which illuminated Peter there, and also James and John? And where will that star rise, but "in your hearts"?[48]

Do you not see how this light shines even now in the hearts of the faithful and perfect? Do you not see how it is superior to the light of knowledge? It has nothing to do with that which comes from Hellenic studies, which is not worthy to be called light, being but deception or confounded with deception, and nearer to darkness than light. Indeed, this light of contemplation even differs from the light that comes from the holy Scriptures, whose light may be compared to "a lamp that shines in an obscure place", whereas the light of mystical contemplation is compared to the star of the morning which shines in full daylight, that is to say, to the sun.[49]

20

But the enemies of such an illumination and such a light also claim that all the lights which God has manifested to the saints are only symbolic apparitions, allusions to immaterial and intelligible realities, shown forth in the imagination through God's providence in particular circumstances, falsely alleging that St. Denys the Areopagite is in agreement with them. In fact the latter states very clearly that the light which illuminated the disciples at the most holy Transfiguration will continually and endlessly dazzle us "with its most brilliant rays" in the Age to Come,[50] when we will be "always with the Lord", according to His promise.[51] For how could this light, so radiant and divine, eternal, supereminently possessing immutable being, have anything in common with all those symbols and allusions which are adapted to particular circumstances, which come into existence only to disappear again, which at one time exist and at another do not exist, or rather, sometimes appear, yet without possessing any true existence?

Think of the sun, which is more resplendent than any other sensible thing, and yet derives its origin from change, and is subject to various annual alterations, with numerous other heavenly bodies interposing themselves in front of it; which sometimes is eclipsed or hidden, yet also indeed obeys at times the orders of saints and consequently alters the direction of its movement, going backwards or stopping in its course.[52] Let us say that this sun and the light that comes from it possess proper being and existence. What then shall we say of that light which admits neither movement nor shadow of change, which is the splendour of the deified flesh,[53] flesh which enriches and communicates the glory of the divinity? Shall we say that this light, the beauty of the eternal Age to Come, is only a symbol, an illusion, something without true existence? Certainly not, as long as we remain lovers of this light.

33

Since the Reality which transcends every intellectual power is impossible to comprehend, it is beyond all beings; such union with God is thus beyond all knowledge, even if it be called "knowledge" metaphorically, nor is it intelligible, even if it be called so. For how can what is beyond all intellect be called intelligible? In respect of its transcendence, it might better be called ignorance than knowledge. It cannot be a part or aspect of knowledge, just as the Superessential is not an aspect of the essential. Knowledge as a whole could not contain it, nor could this knowledge, when subdivided, possess it as one of its parts.

It can in fact be possessed by a kind of ignorance rather than knowledge. For by reason of its transcendence, it is also ignorance, or rather it is beyond ignorance. This union, then, is a unique reality. For whatever name one gives to it—union, vision, sense perception, knowledge, intellection, illumination—would not, properly speaking, apply to it, or else would properly apply to it alone.[54]

35

What then is this union which, by virtue of its transcendence, is not to be identified with any being? Is it apophatic theology? But it has to do with union and not negation. Moreover, to theologise negatively, we do not need to go out from ourselves, whereas to enter into this union, even the angels must go out from themselves.[55] Moreover, while it is true that one who does not theologise by negation is not orthodox, even among the orthodox, only the deiform can attain this union. Again, we have an understanding of apophatic theology and express it verbally; but the great Denys has told us that this union is indescribable and inconceivable even to those who behold it.[56] Also, the light of apophatic theology is nothing more than a kind of knowledge and rational discourse, whereas the light beheld in this contemplation possesses objective reality:[57] It operates intellectually and converses spiritually and ineffably with the one who is being deified.

The mind which applies itself to apophatic theology thinks of what is different from God. Thus it proceeds by means of discursive reasoning. But in the other case, there is union. In the one case, the mind negates itself together with other beings, but in the other there is a union of the mind with God. It is of this that the Fathers speak when they say, "The end of prayer is to be snatched away to God."[58] This is why the great Denys says that through prayer, we are united to God.[59] For in prayer, the mind gradually abandons all relation with created things: first with all things evil and bad, then with neutral things capable of conformity to either good or ill, according to the intentions of the person using them. It is to this last category that all studies belong and the knowledge that comes through them.[60] Hence the Fathers warn us against accepting the knowledge that comes from the Enemy at the time of prayer, so as not to be deprived of that which is superior.[61]

Thus the mind slowly abandons all relation with these things, and even with those superior to them, in order to be totally separated from all beings through pure prayer. This ecstasy is incomparably higher than negative theology, for it belongs only to those who have attained impassibility.[62] But it is not yet union, unless the Paraclete illumines from on high the man who attains in prayer the stage which is superior to the highest natural possibilities, and who is awaiting the promise of the Father; and by His revelation ravishes him to the contemplation of the light.

This contemplation has a beginning, and something follows on from this beginning, more or less dark or clear; but there is never an end, since its progress is infinite, just as is the ravishment in revelation.[63] There is a difference between illumination and a durable vision of light, and the vision of things in the light, whereby even things far off are accessible to the eyes, and the future is shown as already existing.

36

But I am incapable of expressing and explaining these matters. If the preceding topics are equally inexplicable,[64] yet these relate to the subject which concerns us. So to return—the contemplation of this light is a union, even though it does not endure with the imperfect.[65] But is the union with this light other than a vision? And since it is brought about by the cessation of intellectual activity, how could it be accomplished if not by the Spirit?[66]

For it is in light that the light is seen, and that which sees operates in a similar light, since this faculty has no other way in which to work.[67] Having separated itself from all other beings, it becomes itself all light and is assimilated to what it sees, or rather, it is united to it without mingling, being itself light and seeing light through light. If it sees itself, it sees light; if it beholds the object of its vision, that too is light; and if it looks at the means by which it sees, again it is light. For such is the character of the union, that all is one, so that he who sees can distinguish neither the means nor the object nor its nature, but simply has the awareness of being light and of seeing a light distinct from every creature.

37

This is why the great Paul after his extraordinary rapture declared himself ignorant of what it was.[68] Nonetheless, he saw himself. How? By sense perception, by the reason, or by the spiritual intellect?[69] But in his rapture he had transcended these faculties. He therefore saw himself by the Spirit, who had brought about the rapture. But what was he himself, since he was inaccessible to every natural power,[70] or rather deprived of all such power? He was that to which he was united, by which he knew himself, and for which he had detached himself from all else. Such, then, was his union with the light. Even the angels could not attain to this state, at least not without transcending themselves by unifying grace.[71]

Paul therefore *was* light and spirit, to which he was united, by which he had received the capacity of union, having gone out from all beings, and become light by grace, and nonbeing by transcendence, that is by exceeding created things. As St. Maximus says, he who is in God has left behind him "all that is after God ... all the realities, names and values which are after[72] God will be outside those who come to be in God by grace".[73] But in attaining this condition, the divine Paul could not participate absolutely in the divine essence,[74] for the essence of God goes beyond even nonbeing by reason of transcendence, since it is also "more-than-God".[75]

But there is also a "not-being by transcendence"[76] spiritually visible to the senses of the soul, which is definitely not the divine essence, but a glory and radiance inseparable from His nature, by which He unites Himself only to those worthy, whether angels or men. And since angels as much as men see God in this fashion, being united to God and singing hymns to Him, it is probable that if even an angel were to explain this supernatural vision, he would say, much as did Paul: "I know an angel who saw, but I do not know if it was an angel, God knows."[77] How could anyone who recognises the infinite majesty of God, and the heights to which in His love for men He has elevated our lowliness, how could such a man claim that these visions of the saints—which are known only to God and to those to whom they have been revealed, as Gregory the Theologian says[78]—are sensory and, being sensory, are imaginary and symbolic, and human knowledge?[79]

66

This knowledge, which is beyond conception, is common to all who have believed in Christ. As to the goal of this true faith, which comes about by the fulfilling of the commandments, it does not bestow knowledge of God through beings alone, whether knowable or unknowable, for by "beings" here we understand "created things"; but it does so through that uncreated light which is the glory of God, of Christ our God, and of those who attain the supreme goal of being conformed to Christ. For it is in the glory of the Father that Christ will come again, and it is in the glory of their father,[80] Christ, that "the just will shine like the sun";[81] they will be light, and will see the light, a sight delightful and all-holy, belonging only to the purified heart. This light at present shines in part, as a pledge,[82] for those who through impassibility have passed beyond all that is condemned, and through pure and immaterial prayer have passed beyond all that is pure. But on the Last Day, it will deify in a *manifest* fashion "the sons of the Resurrection",[83] who will rejoice in eternity and in glory in communion with Him Who has endowed our nature with a glory and splendour that is divine.

Even in the created realm, this glory and splendour do not pertain to essence.[84] How, then, could one think that the glory of God is the essence of God, of that God who while remaining imparticipable, invisible and impalpable, becomes participable by His superessential power, and communicates Himself and shines forth and becomes in contemplation "One Spirit"[85] with those who meet Him with a pure heart, according to the most mystical and mysterious prayer which our common father addressed to His own Father? "Grant them," He says, "that as I am in you, Father, and you in me, so they too may be one in us", in truth.[86]

Such is the vision of God which in the Age which is without end will be seen only by those judged worthy of such a blessed fulfillment. This same vision was seen in the present age by the chosen among the apostles on Thabor, by Stephen when he was being stoned,[87] and by Anthony in his battle for inner stillness[88]—indeed by the saints, that is, the pure in heart, as one can learn if one wishes from their own written lives and biographies.

I would also affirm that the prophets and patriarchs were not without experience of this light, but that (with a few exceptions) all their visions, especially the most divine ones, have participated in this light. For indeed, why should God have simulated some other light, when He possesses the eternal light in Himself, made visible (albeit in a mysterious way) to the pure in heart today just as in the Age to Come, as the great Denys affirms?[89] Since such is the vision of God, how could He Who said, "Blessed are the pure in heart" not have promised it for eternity, but promised only the knowledge that comes from creatures and can also belong to the wise of this age?

68

It is time to repeat those divine words: "We give thanks to You, Father, Lord of heaven and earth, because", uniting Yourself to us and making Yourself manifest to us by Yourself, "You have hidden these things from the wise and prudent",[90] who are prudent only by their own account and learned only in their own eyes. This is why, when they hear the words of the saints, they reject some and give a false interpretation to others, and sometimes dare even to falsify certain passages to deceive everyone. So, when Gregory of Nyssa explains what is the nature of the contemplation of God granted to the pure in heart, he says, "It is possible also for the wise of this age to obtain a notion of God from the harmony of the world"; however, he then adds, "But, in my opinion, the nobility of the Beatitude suggests another meaning."[91]

Denys the great Areopagite indeed asks how we know God "since He is neither intelligible nor sensible", adding, in a tentative manner, "perhaps it is true to say we know Him not from His own nature but from the dispensation of created things."[92] But he then goes on to reveal to us that most divine knowledge according to the supernatural union with the superluminous light, which comes to pass in a manner beyond mind and knowledge.[93] But these people have ignored the supra-intellectual knowledge as if it did not exist. They have not thought to investigate the reason why Denys expresses himself in a tentative way, as if he had done so from no particular motive; and they have given prominence to this phrase, taken out of context, as if it affirmed that God is known only through His creatures. Our philosopher, Barlaam, has failed to remark that the saint is speaking here of that human knowledge which belongs to all by nature, not of that given by the Spirit. In fact, he is saying, since everyone possesses sense and intelligence as natural faculties, how can these faculties permit us to know God Who is neither sensible nor intelligible?

By another way, certainly, than that of sensible and intelligible beings; these faculties, in short, constitute the means of knowing created beings, but are limited in scope to such beings and manifest God through them.[94] But those who possess not only the faculties of sensation and intellection, but have also obtained spiritual and supernatural grace, do not gain knowledge only through created beings, but also know spiritually, in a manner beyond sense and intelligence, that God is spirit, for they have become entirely God, and know God in God. It is therefore by this mystical knowledge that divine things must be conceived, as the same St. Denys reminds us,[95] and not by natural faculties. We must transcend ourselves altogether, and give ourselves entirely to God,[96] for it is better to belong to God, and not to ourselves. It is thus that divine things are bestowed on those who have attained to fellowship with God.

E.   The uncreated Glory

9

Such a divine and heavenly life belongs to those who live in a manner agreeable to God, participating in the inseparable life of the Spirit, such as Paul himself lived, "the divine and eternal life of Him Who indwelt him", as St. Maximus puts it.[1] Such a life always exists, subsisting in the very nature of the Spirit, Who by nature deifies from all eternity. It is properly called "Spirit" and "divinity" by the saints, in-so-much as the deifying gift[2] is never separate from the Spirit Who gives it. It is a light bestowed in a mysterious illumination, and recognised only by those worthy to receive it.

It is "enhypostatic", not because it possesses a hypostasis of its own, but because the Spirit "sends it out into the hypostasis of another",[3] in which it is indeed contemplated. It is then properly called "enhypostatic", in that it is not contemplated by itself, nor in essence, but in hypostasis.[4] . . . But the Holy Spirit transcends the deifying life which is in Him and proceeds from Him, for it is its own natural energy,[5] which is akin to Him, even if not exactly so. For it is said, "We do not see any deification nor any life exactly similar to the Cause which goes beyond all things in its sublime transcendence."[6] . . . But the Spirit does not only transcend it as Cause, but also in the measure to which what is received is only a part of what is given, for he who receives the divine energy cannot contain it entirely.[7] Thus there are diverse ways in which God transcends such a light, such an uncreated illumination and such a life which is similar to them.

71

10

The inspired Symeon Metaphrastes has composed, on the basis on the first book of Macarius the Great, treatises divided into chapters on the subject of this light and glory, giving a detailed, harmonious and clear interpretation.[8] There can be no better way of contributing to the subject under discussion than to present here some of these chapters in an abridged version.

In chapter 62, he says: "The blessed Moses, by virtue of the glory of the Spirit which shone on his face, and which no man could bear to gaze upon, showed by this sign how the bodies of the saints would be glorified after the resurrection of the righteous. This same glory the faithful souls of the saints will be judged worthy of receiving even now in the inner man, for we contemplate the glory of the Lord with unveiled face";[9] that is, in the inner man, "transfigured from glory to glory according to the same image."[10]

And in chapter 63 he adds: "The glory which even now enriches the souls of the saints will cover and clothe their naked bodies after the resurrection, and will elevate them to the heavens, clad in the glory of their good deeds and of the Spirit; that glory which the souls of the saints have received now in part, as I have said. Thus, glorified by the divine light, the saints will be always with the Lord."[11]

According to the great Denys, that was the same light which illumined the chosen apostles on the Mountain: "When we become incorruptible and immortal," he says, "and attain to the blessed state of conformity with Christ, we will be ever with the Lord (as Scripture says),[12] gaining fulfillment in the purest contemplations of His visible theophany which will illuminate us with its most brilliant rays, just as it illuminated the disciples at the time of the most divine Transfiguration."[13]

This is the light of God, as John has said in his *Apocalypse*,[14] and such is the opinion of all the saints. As Gregory the Theologian remarked, "In my view, he will come as he appeared or was manifested to the disciples on the Mountain, the divine triumphing over the corporeal."[15]

11

"But," Barlaam says, "this light was a sensible light, visible through the medium of the air, appearing to the amazement of all and then at once disappearing. One calls it 'divinity' because it is a symbol of divinity." What a novel opinion! How can one speak of a sensible and created divinity which lasts only a day, appearing only to disappear on the same day, rather like those creatures one calls ephemeral?[16] In fact, it lasts even less long than they do, since it occurs and disappears in a single hour; it would be better to say it once appeared but never existed.[17] Can this be the divinity which (without ever being the true divinity) triumphed over that venerable flesh akin to God?[18] One should not say it triumphed for one minute, but does so continually, for Gregory did not say "having triumphed", but "triumphing", that is, not only in the present but also in the Age to Come.[19]

What do you say to this? Is it to such a divinity that the Lord will be united, and in which He will triumph for endless ages? And will God be all in all for us, as the apostles and Fathers proclaim,[20] when in the case of Christ, divinity will be replaced by a sensible light? According to the same patristic testimony, "We will need neither air nor space nor any such thing"[21] in order to see Him; how then will we see Him by the medium of the air?

Why in the Age to Come should we have more symbols of this kind, more mirrors, more enigmas? Will the vision face-to-face remain still in the realm of hope?[22] For indeed if even in heaven there are still to be symbols, mirrors, enigmas, then we have been deceived in our hopes, deluded by sophistry; thinking that the promise will make us acquire the true divinity, we do not even gain a vision of divinity. A sensible light replaces this, whose nature is entirely foreign to God! How can this light be a symbol, and if it is, how can it be called divinity? For the drawing of a man is not humanity, nor is the symbol of an angel the nature of an angel.

12

What saint has ever said that this light was a created symbol? Gregory the Theologian says, "It was as light that the divinity was manifested to the disciples on the Mountain."[23] So, if the light was not really the true divinity, but its created symbol, one would have to say, not that the divinity manifested was light, but that light caused the divinity to appear. . . . Similarly, Chrysostom states that the Lord showed himself in greater splendour when the divinity manifested its rays. Note here the article: He says not "divinity" simply, but "*the* divinity", the true Godhead.[24] And how could it be a question of "rays of the divinity" if the light was only a symbol of divinity, formed from another nature?[25]

Again, Basil the Great, after showing that the God Who is adored in three Persons is a unique light, speaks of the "God who dwells in light unapproachable",[26] for the unapproachable is in every way true, and the true unapproachable. This is why the apostles fell to the ground, unable to rest their gaze on the glory of the light of the Son, because it was a "light unapproachable". The Spirit, too, is light, as we read: "He who has shone in our hearts by the Holy Spirit."[27]

If then the unapproachable is true and this light was unapproachable, the light was not a simulacrum of divinity, but truly the light of the true divinity, not only the divinity of the Son, but that of the Father and the Spirit too. This is why we sing together to the Lord when we celebrate the annual Feast of the Transfiguration: "In Your light which appeared today on Thabor, we have seen the Father as light and also the Spirit as light,"[28] for "You have unveiled an indistinct ray of Your divinity."[29] ... So, when all the saints agree in calling this light true divinity, how do you dare to consider it alien to the divinity, calling it "a created reality", and "a symbol of divinity", and claiming that it is inferior to our intellection?

13

Maximus, who is accustomed to reason by symbols, analogies and allegories, does not (as you know) always use the inferior as symbol of the superior, but sometimes the opposite: Thus he can say that the body of the Lord hanging on the Cross has become the symbol of our body nailed to the passions.[30] Similarly, Maximus, speaking allegorically, claimed that this light was a symbol of the cataphatic and apophatic theologies;[31] he spoke of a superior reality as the symbol of inferior ones, a reality which contains in itself the knowledge of theology, and is its source.

Did he not also say that Moses is the symbol of providence and Elijah of judgement?[32] Are we for that reason to assume these prophets never really existed, but all was fantasy and imagination? Who else but Barlaam would have dared to say so, or claim that this light was a nature alien to the divinity, a simulacrum of divinity? This is why the choir of inspired theologians have almost all been chary of calling the grace of this light simply a symbol, so that people should not be led astray by the ambiguity of this term to conclude that this most divine light is a created reality, alien to the divinity.[33] Neverthe-less, the phrase "symbol of divinity", wisely and properly under-stood, cannot be considered absolutely opposed to the truth.

14

But let us then suppose it is a symbol of divinity, as you believe. Even so, you will not utterly convince us of error nor deprive us of our blessed hope. For every symbol either derives from the nature of the object of which it is a symbol, or belongs to an entirely different nature. Thus, when the sun is about to rise, the dawn is a natural symbol of its light, and similarly heat is a natural symbol of the burn-ing power of fire.[34]

As to signs which are not connatural in this way, and which have their own independent existence, they are sometimes considered sym-bols: Thus, a burning torch might be taken as a symbol of attacking enemies. If they do not possess their own natural existence, they can serve as a kind of phantom to foretell the future, and then the symbol consists only in that. Such were the perceptible signs shown by the prophets in simple figures, for example, the scythe of Zachariah,[35] the axes of Ezekiel,[36] and other signs of this sort.

So a natural symbol always accompanies the nature which gives them being, for the symbol is natural to that nature; as for the symbol which derives from another nature, having its own existence, it is quite impossible for it constantly to be associated with the object it symbolises, for nothing prevents it from existing before and after this object, like any reality having its own existence. Finally, the symbol lacking an independent existence exists neither before nor after its object, for that is impossible; as soon as it has appeared, it at once is dissolved into nonbeing and disappears completely.

Thus if the light of Thabor is a symbol, it is either a natural or a nonnatural one. If the latter, then it either has its own existence or is just a phantom without subsistence. But if it is merely an insubstan-tial phantom, then Christ never really was, is or will be such as He appeared on Thabor. Yet Denys the Areopagite, Gregory the Theolo-gian and all the others who await His coming from heaven with glo-ry, affirm clearly that Christ will be for all eternity as He then appeared, as we showed above.[37] This light, then, is not just a phan-tom without subsistence.

15

Indeed, not only will Christ be eternally thus in the future, but He was such even before He ascended the Mountain. Hear John Damascene, who is wise in divine things: "Christ is transfigured, not by putting on some quality He did not possess previously, nor by changing into something He never was before, but by revealing to His disciples what He truly was, in opening their eyes and in giving sight to those who were blind. For while remaining identical to what He had been before, He appeared to the disciples in His splendour; He is indeed the true light, the radiance of glory."[38]

Basil the Great testifies to the same truth: "His divine power appeared as it were as a light through a screen of glass, that is to say, through the flesh of the Lord which He had assumed from us; the power which enlightens those who have purified the eyes of the heart."[39] And do not the annual hymns of the Church affirm that, even before the Transfiguration, He had previously been such as He then appeared? "What appeared today was hidden by the flesh, and the original beauty, more than resplendent, has been unveiled today."[40]

Moreover, the transformation of our human nature, its deification and transfiguration—were these not accomplished in Christ from the start, from the moment in which He assumed our nature?[41] Thus He was divine before, but He bestowed at the time of His Transfiguration a divine power upon the eyes of the apostles and enabled them to look up and see for themselves.[42] This light, then, was not a hallucination but will remain for eternity, and has existed from the beginning.

16

But if Christ was such and will remain such for eternity, He is also still the same today. It would indeed be absurd to believe that such was His nature up to the most divine vision on Thabor, and that it will always be such in the Age to Come, but that it has become different in the intervening period, setting aside this glory. Today also He is seated in the same splendour, "at the right hand of the Majesty on high".[43] All then must follow and obey Him Who says, "Come, let us ascend the holy and heavenly mountain, let us contemplate the immaterial divinity of the Father and the Spirit, which shines forth in the only Son."[44] And if one refuses to be convinced by a single saint, one may be obedient to two, or rather all. So the blessed Andrew, who was as a shining and holy lamp in Crete, thus hymns the light which shone on Thabor: "The intelligible world of angels, in celebrating this light in an immaterial manner, gives us a proof of the love which the Word bears towards us."[45]

The great Denys says almost the same thing when celebrating the sublime order of supercosmic powers:[46] They do not only contemplate and participate in the glory of the Trinity, he declares, but also in the glorification of Jesus. Having been made worthy of this contemplation, they are also initiated into it, for He Himself is deifying light: "They truly draw near to it, and gain first participation in the knowledge of His theurgic light."[47] Macarius similarly states . . ., "Our mixed human nature, which was assumed by the Lord, has taken its seat on the right hand of the divine majesty in the heavens,[48] being full of glory not only(like Moses) in the face, but in the whole body."[49]

Therefore Christ possesses this light immutably, or rather, He has always possessed it, and always will have it with Him. But if it always was, is and will be, then the light which glorified the Lord on the Mountain was not a hallucination, nor simply a symbol without subsistence.

17

And if someone says that this light is an independent reality, separate from the nature of Him Whom it signifies, of Whom it is only a symbol—then let him show where and of what kind this reality is, which is shown by experience to be unapproachable, and not only to the eyes ("The disciples fell head-first to the ground",[50] we are told), and which shone forth only from the venerated face and body of Christ. For otherwise, if it *were* an independent reality, eternally associated with Christ in the Age to Come, He would be composed of three natures and three essences: the human, the divine and that of this light. So it is obvious and clearly demonstrated that this light is neither an independent reality, nor something alien to the divinity.

Having reached this point in our treatise, we must now explain why the saints call this deifying grace and divine light "enhypostatic".

18

Clearly, this term is not used to affirm that it possesses its own hypostasis.[51] ... By contrast, one calls "*an*hypostatic" not only non-being or hallucination, but also everything which quickly disintegrates and runs away, which disappears and straightway ceases to be, such as, for example, thunder and lightning, and our own words and thoughts. The Fathers have done well, then, to call this light *en*hypostatic, in order to show its permanence and stability, because it remains in being, and does not elude the gaze, as does lightning, or words, or thoughts. ... [52]

19

If then this light, which shone from the Saviour on the Mountain, is a natural symbol, it is not so in respect of *both* the natures in Him, for the natural characteristics of each nature are different.[53] This light cannot pertain to His human nature, for our nature is not light, let alone a light such as this. The Saviour did not ascend Thabor, accompanied by the chosen disciples, in order to show them that He was a man. For during the three years previous to this, they had seen Him living with them and taking part in their way of life; as Scripture puts it, "in company" with them.[54] No, He went up to show them "that he was the radiance of the Father".[55] In view of this, no one could say the light was a symbol of his humanity. If then it was a natural symbol ... this light naturally symbolises the *divinity* of the Only Begotten, as John of Damascus has clearly taught: "The Son eternally begotten of the Father possesses the natural and eternal ray of divinity; yet the glory of the divinity has become also the glory of the body."[56] This glory did not appear or begin, it has no end, for natural symbols are always coexistent with the natures of which they are symbols. ... As Maximus says, "All the realities which are by essence contemplated around God have neither beginning nor end."[57] But since as he says, these realities ... are numerous yet in no way diminish the notion of simplicity, no more will this luminous symbol (which is one of them) cause any detriment to the simple nature of God.[58]

20

Many other sources, in particular the liturgical hymns, confirm that this light is one of the realities contemplated around God. Let this example suffice: "On the holy Mountain, O Christ, You showed the splendour of Your divine and essential beauty, hidden under the flesh, and enlightened, O Benefactor, the disciples who accompanied You."[59] Also, the remark of Maximus, that "on account of His love of men, He became His own symbol",[60] shows that this light is a natural symbol.

In the realm of nonnatural symbols, an object can be the symbol of another, but not its own symbol.[61] But when the symbol naturally takes its being from the object of which it is the symbol, we say it is its own symbol. The capacity of fire to burn, which has as its symbol the heat accessible to the senses, becomes its own symbol, for it is always accompanied by this heat, yet remains a single entity, not undergoing any duplication; but it always uses heat as its natural symbol, whenever an object capable of receiving heat presents itself.

In the same way, the light of the rising sun has as symbol the glow of the dawn, which becomes its own proper symbol. We all know the sun's light as something accessible to sight, which also enables us to behold the dawn, even though no one can look directly at the solar disc, and it is almost impossible to gaze upon its brilliance.

Similarly, through the sense of touch, a man perceives the warmth of fire, even though touch cannot have the least knowledge of the burning power of which the heat is symbol (although it is well aware that this is the case). It knows neither its quality, nor its intensity, and would in fact perish (becoming itself all fire, and ceasing to be the perceiving subject), if it tried itself to learn by experience what is the nature of the power of fire which gives rise to the heat. This is why, if it should ever venture to attempt this, it would at once shrink back and run away, bitterly regretting its curiosity. So we see that heat is accessible to the touch, but its burning power remains entirely beyond participation.[62]

21

If such is the case, how could one say that the divinity, transcendent in mysteries, becomes knowable the moment its natural symbol is known? What, then? If the dawn, symbol of the light of day, were to remain unapproachable to human eyes, as does the sun (or even more inaccessible than that), how could our eyes see the day and behold other objects in the light of day? How could they know of what kind is the light of the sun which is analogous to that of the day?[63]

Even more are divine things recognised by participation only, since no one (not even the sublime supracosmic intelligences)[64] knows what they are in their ground of being and principle of existence; for our own part, we are certainly far from knowing these things.

22

However, the disciples would not even have seen the symbol, had they not first received eyes they did not possess before.[65] As John of Damascus puts it, "From being blind men, they began to see",[66] and to contemplate this uncreated light. The light, then, became accessible to their eyes, but to eyes which saw in a way superior to that of natural sight, and had acquired the spiritual power of the spiritual light. This mysterious light, inaccessible, immaterial, uncreated, deifying, eternal, this radiance of the Divine Nature, this glory of the divinity, this beauty of the heavenly kingdom, is at once accessible to sense perception and yet transcends it.[67] Does such a reality really seem to you to be a symbol alien to divinity, sensible, created and "visible through the medium of air"?[68]

Listen again to Damascene's assertion that the light is not alien but natural to the divinity. "The splendour of divine grace is not something external, as in the case of the splendour possessed by Moses, but belongs to the very nature of the divine glory and splendour."[69] And again: "In the age to come, we will be always with the Lord,[70] and contemplate Christ resplendent in the light of the Godhead, a light victorious over every nature."[71] And again: "He takes with Him the leaders of the apostles as witnesses of His own glory and divinity, and reveals to them His own divinity", which transcends all things, unique, utterly perfect and anticipating the End.[72]

That this light is not visible through the mediation of air is shown by the great Denys,[73] and those who with him call it the "light of the age to come", an age in which we will no longer need air. Basil the Great similarly states that it is visible to the eyes of the heart. The fact that it is not visible through the medium of air shows us it is not a sensible light. Indeed, when it was shining on Thabor more brilliantly than the sun, the people of the area did not even see it! . . .

23

Do you still insist that the light of the divine and essential beauty is not only sensible and created, but also inferior to our intellection?[74] Heavens above! Are those also inferior to our intellection who see in themselves the light of the divine kingdom, the beauty of the Age to Come, the glory of the Divine Nature? This same light was seen by the apostles, after they had transcended every sensible and intellectual perception, and had received (in the words of Andrew of Crete) "the faculty of truly seeing by virtue of seeing nothing, and had acquired the sense of the supernatural by experiencing divine things".[75] Since in such a case, an ecstasy inferior to intellection is demonic, is it then a demonic ecstasy which those initiated by the Lord have experienced?[76] How unthinkable! On the contrary, we have learnt to sing together to Christ: "The chosen apostles were transformed by the divine ecstasy on the Mountain, contemplating the irresistible outpouring of Your light and Your unapproachable Divinity."[77]

You might as well claim that God is a creature, as declare that His essential energies are created! For no intelligent man would say that the essential goodness and life *are* the superessential essence of God. The essential characteristic is not the essence which possesses the essential characteristics. As the great Denys says, "When we call the superessential Mystery 'God' or 'life' or 'essence', we have in mind only the providential powers produced from the imparticipable God."[78] These, then, are the essential powers; as to the Superessential ... that is the Reality which possesses these powers and gathers them into unity in itself. Similarly, the deifying light is also essential, but is not itself the essence of God.[79]

24

Our philosopher is not content to stop here, but goes on to claim that every power and energy of God is created. But the saints clearly teach that all the natural characteristics, all the power and energy of the uncreated nature are themselves uncreated, just as those of a created nature are created.

"But how can it be," asks Barlaam, "that a Reality that transcends the senses and mind, which is Being *par excellence*, eternal, immaterial, unchangeable—what you call 'enhypostatic' is not the Superessential essence of God, since it bears the characteristics of the Master, and transcends every visible and invisible creature? Why do you say the essence of God transcends this light?"[80] ... He alleges that the description that fits us best is "ditheist",[81] even though he admits ... that we hold that there is only one Reality that transcends all things, and that this is the Superessential; and so, according to him, we teach that there is only one God, and that this light is not an essence, but an energy of the divine essence, concerning which essence we state that it is unique and transcends all as working in all.

But even if we affirm that this energy is inseparable from the unique divine essence, the Superessential is not for that reason composite; without doubt, no simple essence would exist if it were so, for one would search in vain for a natural essence without energy.[82] How is it possible for the deifying light not to bear the Master's characteristics?

... And since the saints speak here of an enhypostatic Reality, but not of an hypostasis existing on its own, how could the light be an independent essence or a second God, since it does not possess an independent existence? And if you are led to posit another God, on the pretext that this energy is unoriginate, uncreated and not intelligible, then you must also hold that the will of God constitutes a second God. As Maximus says, "The divine nature in three hypostases is entirely unoriginate, uncreated, not intelligible, simple and without composition, and so similarly is its will."[83] And the same could be said of all the natural energies belonging to the divinity.[84]

26

You claim that the grace of deification is a natural state, that is, the activity and manifestation of a natural power. Without realising it, you are falling into the error of the Messalians, for the deified man would necessarily be God by nature, if deification depended on our natural powers, and was included among the laws of nature![85] ... But know that the grace of deification transcends every natural relationship, and there does not exist in nature "any faculty capable of receiving it."[86]

For if it were no longer a grace, but a manifestation of the energy which appertains to natural power, there would be nothing absurd in holding that deification occurred according to the measure of the receptive power of nature. Deification would then be a work of nature, not a gift of God, and the deified man would be god by nature and receive the name of "God" in the proper sense. For the natural power of each thing is simply the continuous activation of nature.[87] But in that case, I cannot understand why deification should cause a man to go out from himself,[88] if it is itself subject to the laws of nature.

27

The grace of deification thus transcends nature, virtue and knowledge, and (as St. Maximus says) "all these things are inferior to it".[89] Every virtue and imitation of God on our part indeed prepares those who practise them for divine union, but the mysterious union itself is effected by grace. It is through grace that "the entire Divinity comes to dwell in fulness in those deemed worthy",[90] and all the saints in their entire being dwell in God, receiving God in His wholeness, and gaining no other reward for their ascent to Him than God Himself. "He is conjoined to them as a soul is to its body, to its own limbs";[91] judging it right to dwell in believers by the authentic adoption, according to the gift and grace of the Holy Spirit. So, when you hear that God dwells in us through the virtues, or that by means of the memory He comes to be established in us,[92] do not imagine that deification is simply the possession of the virtues; but rather that it resides in the radiance and grace of God, which really comes to us through the virtues. As St. Basil the Great says, "A soul which has curbed its natural impulses by a personal *ascesis* and the help of the Holy Spirit, becomes worthy (according to the just judgment of God) of the splendour granted to the saints."[93]

The splendour granted by the grace of God is light, as you may learn from this text: "The splendour for those who have been purified is light, for the just will shine like the sun;[94] God will stand in the midst of them,[95] distributing and determining the dignities of blessedness, for they are gods and kings."[96] No one will deny that this relates to supracelestial and supracosmic realities, for "it is possible to receive the supracelestial light among the promises of good things". Solomon declares, "Light shines always for the just",[97] and the Apostle Paul says, "We give thanks to God who has counted us worthy to participate in the heritage of the saints in light."[98]

28

We said earlier that wisdom comes to man through effort and study; not that it is *only* effort and study, but that it is the result of these. The Lord dwells in men in different and varied ways according to the worthiness and way of life of those who seek Him. He appears in one way to an active man, in another to a contemplative, in another again to the man of vision, and in yet different ways to the zealous or to those already divinised. There are numerous differences in the divine vision itself: Among the prophets, some have seen God in a dream, others when awake by means of enigmas and mirrors; but to Moses He appeared "face-to-face, and not in enigmas."[99]

But when you hear of the vision of God face-to-face, recall the testimony of Maximus: "Deification is an enhypostatic[100] and direct illumination which has no beginning, but appears in those worthy as something exceeding their comprehension. It is indeed a mystical union with God, beyond intellect and reason, in the age when creatures will no longer know corruption. Thanks to this union, the saints, observing the light of the hidden and more-than-ineffable glory, become themselves able to receive the blessed purity, in company with the celestial powers. Deification is also the invocation of the great God and Father, the symbol of the authentic and real adoption, according to the gift and grace of the Holy Spirit, thanks to the bestowal of which grace the saints become and will remain the sons of God."[101]

29

The great Denys, who elsewhere terms this light a "superluminous and theurgic ray",[102] also calls it "deifying gift and principle of the Divinity",[103] that is to say, of deification. To one who asks how God can transcend the thearchy (that is to say, the very principle of the divinity), he replies:[104] You have heard that God permits Himself to be seen face-to-face, not in enigmas,[105] that He becomes attached to those worthy as is a soul to its body, to its own members; that He unites Himself to them to the extent of dwelling completely in them, so that they too dwell entirely in Him; that "through the Son, the Spirit is poured out in abundance on us",[106] not as something created, and that we participate in Him, and He speaks through us—all this you know. But you should not consider that God allows Himself to be seen in His superessential essence, but according to His deifying gift and energy, the grace of adoption, the uncreated deification, the enhypostatic illumination. You should think that that is the principle of the divinity, the deifying gift, in which one may supernaturally communicate, which one may see and with which one may be united.

But the essence of God, which is beyond principle, transcends this principle, too.

This grace is in fact a relationship, albeit not a natural one; yet it is at the same time beyond relationship, not only by virtue of being supernatural, but also *qua* relationship. For how would a relationship have a relationship? But as to the essence of God, that is unrelated, not *qua* relationship, but because it transcends the supernatural relationships themselves. Grace is communicated to all worthy of it, in a way proper and peculiar to each one, while the divine essence transcends all that is participable.[107]

30

He who says[108] "the deifying gift is a state of perfection of the rational nature, which has existed since the first disposition of the world and finds its fulfillment in the most elevated of the rational beings", manifestly opposes himself to Christ's Gospel. If deification does no more than perfect the rational nature, without elevating those made in the form of God beyond that condition; if it is only a state of the rational nature, since it is only activated by a natural power, the deified saints do not transcend nature, they are not "born of God",[109] are not "spirit because born of the Spirit",[110] and Christ, by coming into the world, has not "given the power to become children of God" to those alone "who believe in His name".[111] Deification would have belonged to all nations even before He came if it naturally pertains to the rational soul, just as today it would belong to everyone irrespective of faith or piety. For if deification were only the perfection of the rational nature, then the pagan Greeks were not entirely rational, neither are the fallen angels; one cannot charge them with misusing their knowledge, yet they have been deprived of the natural state appropriate to such knowledge. Of what, then, were they really guilty? Even the pagan wise men admit that an essence cannot be more or less essential. How then could an angel or soul be more or less rational?

For imperfection in the case of those not yet mature in years resides not in the nature of the soul, but in that of the body. Is deification then to be identified with the age which brings rational thought? For our part, we consider the fact that some men know more than others belongs not to the nature of the soul, but to the constitution of the body.[112] Is deification then this constitution in its natural state of perfection?

But we know that natural perfection is itself a gift of God, even though knowledge is not only a gift of God, but a state of perfection of the rational nature. However, this state, since it is not supernatural, is not a deifying gift, because the deifying gift is supernatural. Otherwise all men and angels without exception would be more or less gods, and the race of demons would be imperfect gods or demigods. . . . Thus, whatever the state in which the rational nature attains perfection, whether it is a knowledge, a constitution, a natural perfection of body and soul, whether it comes from within them or from outside a man, it can truly make perfect those rational beings who possess it, but it cannot make them gods.[113]

31

But, as we have shown above, the saints clearly state that this adoption, actualised by faith, is enhypostatic.[114] Nonetheless, our opponent affirms that the imitation of God, which he alone considers to be the thearchy and the deifying gift, is not enhypostatic. It is therefore something different from the deification which the Fathers possessed and knew. Yet the divine Maximus has not only taught that it is enhypostatic, but also that it is unoriginate (not only uncreated), indescribable and supratemporal.[115] Those who attain it become thereby uncreated, unoriginate and indescribable, although in their own nature, they derive from nothingness.[116] But this man, intruding upon things of which he is ignorant, claims that deification is created and natural, subject to time; and because he conceives of it according to his own measure, reduces God (together with it) to the level of a creature.

According to the Fathers, deification is an essential energy of God; but any essence of which the essential energies are created must itself necessarily be created![117] . . . Barlaam indeed does not blush to claim that all the powers and natural energies of God are created, even though our faith teaches us that every saint is a temple of God by reason of the grace that indwells him. How could the dwelling place of a creature be a temple of God? How could every saint become uncreated by grace, if this grace is created?

What is most astonishing to me is that he admits that the light which shone forth on Thabor is called "theurgic" light[118] by the Fathers, but refuses to call it a deifying gift. Since the deifying gift of the Spirit is an energy of God, and since the divine names derive from the energies[119] (for the Superessential is nameless), God could not be called "God", if deification consists only in virtue and wisdom! But He is called "God" on the basis of His deifying energy,[120] while wisdom and virtue only manifest this energy. He could no longer be called "More-than-God" by reason of His transcendence in respect of this divinity; it would have to suffice to call Him "more-than-wise", "more-than-good", and so forth.[121] So the grace and energy of deification are different from virtue and wisdom.

32

... When you hear speak of the deifying energy of God and the theurgic grace of the Spirit, do not busy yourself or seek to know why it is this or that and not something else; for without it you cannot be united to God, according to those Fathers who have spoken about it. Attend rather to those works which will allow you to attain to it, for thus you will know it according to your capacities;[122] for, as St. Basil tells us, he alone knows the energies of the Spirit who has learnt of them through *experience*.[123] As for the man who seeks knowledge before works, if he trusts in those who have had the experience, he obtains a certain image of the truth. But if he tries to conceive of it by himself, he finds himself deprived even of the image of truth. He then puffs himself up with pride as if he had discovered it, and breathes forth his anger against the men of experience as if they were in error. Do not be overcurious, therefore, but follow the men of experience in your works, or at least in your words, remaining content with the exterior manifestations of grace.[124]

Deification is in fact beyond every name. This is why we, who have written much about *hesychia* (sometimes at the urging of the fathers, sometimes in response to the questions of the brothers) have never dared hitherto to write about deification. But now, since there is a necessity to speak, we will speak words of piety (by the grace of the Lord), but words inadequate to describe it. For even when spoken about, deification remains ineffable, and (as the Fathers teach us) can be given a name only by those who have received it.[125]

33

The Principle of deification, divinity by nature, the imparticipable Origin whence the deified derive their deification, Beatitude itself, transcendent over all things and supremely thearchic, is itself inaccessible to all sense perception and to every mind, to every incorporeal or corporeal being.[126] It is only when one or another of these beings goes out from itself and acquires a superior state that it is deified. For it is only when hypostatically united to a mind or body that we believe the divinity to have become visible, even though such union transcends the proper nature of mind and body.[127] Only those beings united to It are deified "by the total presence of the Anointer";[128] they have received an energy identical to that of the deifying essence,[129] and possessing it in absolute entirety, reveal it through themselves. For, as the Apostle says, "In Christ the fulness of the divinity dwells bodily."[130]

This is why certain saints after the Incarnation have seen this light as a limitless sea, flowing forth in a paradoxical manner from the unique Sun,[131] that is, from the adorable Body of Christ, as in the case of the apostles on the Mountain. It is thus that the firstfruits[132] of our human constitution are deified. But the deification of divinised angels and men is not the superessential essence of God, but the energy of this essence. This energy does not manifest itself in deified creatures, as art does in the work of art; for it is thus that the creative power manifests itself in the things created by it, becoming thereby universally visible and at the same time reflected in them. On the contrary, deification manifests itself in these creatures "as art in the man who has acquired it", according to Basil the Great.[133]

This is why the saints are the instruments of the Holy Spirit, having received the same energy as He has.[134] As certain proof of what I say, one might cite the charisms of healing, the working of miracles, foreknowledge, the irrefutable wisdom which the Lord called "the spirit of your Father",[135] and also the sanctifying bestowal of the Spirit which those sanctified with these gifts receive from and through them. Thus God said to Moses, "I shall take the spirit which is on you and put it on them";[136] similarly, "when Paul laid his hands" on the twelve Ephesians, "the Holy Spirit came upon them", and at once "they spoke in tongues and prophesied".[137]

Thus when we consider the proper dignity of the Spirit, we see it to be equal to that of the Father and the Son; but when we think of the grace that works in those who partake of the Spirit, we say that the Spirit is in us, "that it is poured out on us, but is not created, that it is given to us but is not made, it is granted but not produced".[138] In the words of the great Basil, it is present in those still imperfect as a certain disposition, "because of the instability of their moral choice", but in those more perfect, as an acquired state, or in some of them, as a fixed state—indeed more than this, "the energy of the Spirit is present in the purified soul as the visual faculty in the healthy eye", as he puts it.[139]

34

The deifying gift of the Spirit thus cannot be equated with the superessential essence of God. It is the deifying energy of this divine essence, yet not the totality of this energy, even though it is indivisible in itself.[140] Indeed, what created thing could receive the entire, infinitely potent power of the Spirit, except He who was carried in the womb of a Virgin, by the presence of the Holy Spirit and the overshadowing of the power of the Most High?[141] He received "all the fulness of the Divinity".[142]

As for us, "it is of *His* fulness that we have all received".[143] The essence of God is everywhere, for, as it is said, "the Spirit fills all things",[144] according to essence. Deification is likewise everywhere, ineffably present in the essence and inseparable from it, as its natural power. But just as one cannot see fire, if there is no matter to receive it, nor any sense organ capable of perceiving its luminous energy, in the same way one cannot contemplate deification if there is no matter to receive the divine manifestation. But if with every veil removed it lays hold of appropriate matter, that is of any purified rational nature, freed from the veil of manifold evil, then it becomes itself visible as a spiritual light, or rather it transforms these creatures into spiritual light.[145] "The prize of virtue," it is said, "is to become God, to be illumined by the purest of lights, by becoming a son of that day which no darkness can dim. For it is another Sun which produces this day, a Sun which shines forth the true light. And once it has illumined us, it no longer hides itself in the West, but envelops all things with its powerful light. It grants an eternal and endless light to those worthy, and transforms those who participate in this light into other suns."[146] Then, indeed, "the just will shine like the sun".[147] What sun? Surely that same one which appears even now to those worthy as it did then.

35

Do you not see that they will acquire the same energy as the Sun of Righteousness? This is why various divine signs and the communication of the Holy Spirit are effected through them. Indeed, it is written: "Just as the air around the earth, driven upwards by the wind, becomes luminous because it is transformed by the purity of the aether, so it is with the human mind which quits this impure and grimy world: it becomes luminous by the power of the Spirit, and mingles with the true and sublime purity; it shines itself in this purity, becoming entirely radiant, transformed into light according to the promise of the Lord, who foretold that the just would shine like the sun."[148]

We can observe the same phenomenon here below with a mirror or a sheet of water: Receiving the sun's ray, they produce another ray from themselves. And we too will become luminous if we lift ourselves up, abandoning earthly shadows, by drawing near to the true light of Christ. And if the true light which "shines in darkness"[149] comes down to us, we will also be light, as the Lord told His disciples.[150]

Thus the deifying gift of the Spirit is a mysterious light, and transforms into light those who receive its richness; He does not only fill them with eternal light, but grants them a knowledge and a life appropriate to God. Thus, as Maximus teaches, Paul lived no longer a created life, but "the eternal life of Him Who indwelt him".[151] Similarly, the prophets contemplated the future as if it were the present.

So the man who has seen God by means not of an alien symbol but by a natural symbol, has truly seen Him in a spiritual way.[152] I do not consider as a natural symbol of God what is only an ordinary symbol, visible or audible by the senses as such, and activated through the medium of the air. When, however, the seeing eye does not see as an ordinary eye, but as an eye opened by the power of the Spirit, it does not see God by the means of an alien symbol; and it is then we can speak of sense-perception transcending the senses.[153]

36

One recognises this light when the soul ceases to give way to the evil pleasures and passions, when it acquires inner peace and the stilling of thoughts, spiritual repose and joy, contempt of human glory, humility allied with a hidden rejoicing, hatred of the world, love of heavenly things, or rather the love of the sole God of Heaven.[154] Moreover, if one covers the eyes of him who sees, even if one gouges them out, he will still see the light no less clearly than before. How then could he be persuaded by someone who claims that this light is visible through the medium of air, and that it is in no way useful to the rational soul, as something belonging to the bodily senses?[155]

But that contemplative, realising full well that he does not see by the senses *qua* senses, may think he sees by the mind. However, a careful examination will cause him to discover that the mind does not apprehend this light by virtue of its own power. Hence our expression, "mind surpassing mind", meaning thereby that a man possessing mind and sense perception sees in a way transcending both of these faculties.

And when you hear the great Denys advising Timothy to "abandon the senses and intellectual activities",[156] do not conclude from this that a man is neither to reason nor see. For he does not lose these faculties, except by amazement. But you should hold that intellectual activities are entirely bypassed by the light of union and by the action of this light.[157] This is clearly shown by Peter, the leader of the apostles and foundation-stone of the Church: At the time of the holy Pentecost, when he was deemed worthy of the mysterious and divine union, he was nonetheless still able to see those who were being illumined and filled with light together with himself, and to hear what they were saying, and was aware what time of day it was ("It is the third hour", he said).[158] For when energy of the Holy Spirit overshadows the human mind, those in whom He is working do not become disturbed in mind, for this would be contrary to the promise of the divine presence. He who receives God does not lose his senses. On the contrary, he becomes like one driven mad, so to speak, by the Spirit of wisdom; for this light is also the wisdom of God, present in the deified man, yet not separate from God. "Through it," we read, "all knowledge is revealed, and God truly makes Himself known to the soul He loves",[159] as He makes known at the same time all justice, holiness and liberty.

As St. Paul says, "Where there is the Spirit of God, there is liberty."[160] And again, "He whom God has made wisdom, justice, sanctification and redemption for us."[161] Hear what St. Basil the Great teaches: "He who has been set in motion by the Spirit has become an eternal movement, a holy creature. For when the Spirit has come to dwell in him, a man receives the dignity of a prophet, of an apostle, of an angel of God, whereas hitherto he was only earth and dust."[162] Hear also John Chrysostom: "The mouth by which God speaks is the mouth of God—for just as our mouth is the mouth of our soul, and the soul does not literally possess a mouth; so likewise the mouth of the prophets is the mouth of God."[163] The Lord too set His seal on this truth, for after saying, "I will give you a mouth, and a wisdom which none of your enemies will be able to gainsay,"[164] He added, "For it is not you who will speak, but the Spirit of your Father who speaks in you."[165]

F. Essence and energies in God

I should like to ask this man why he claims that only the divine essence is without beginning, whereas everything apart from it is of a created nature, and whether or not he thinks this essence is all-powerful. That is to say, does it possess the faculties of knowing, of prescience, of creating, of embracing all things in itself; does it possess providence, the power of deification and, in a word, all such faculties, or not? For if it does not have them, this essence is not God, even though it alone is unoriginate. If it does possess these powers, but acquired them subsequently, then there was a time when it was imperfect, in other words, was not God. However, if it possessed these faculties from eternity, it follows that not only is the divine essence unoriginate, but that each of its powers is also.[1]

Nonetheless, there is only one unoriginate essence, the essence of God; none of the powers that inhere in it is an essence, so that all necessarily and always are *in* the divine essence. To use an obscure image, they exist in the divine essence as do the powers of the senses in what is called the common spiritual sense of the soul.[2] Here is the manifest, sure and recognised teaching of the Church!

For just as there is only one single essence without beginning, the essence of God, and the essences other than it are seen to be of a created nature, and come to be through this sole unoriginate essence, the unique maker of essences—in the same way, there is only one single providential power without beginning, namely that of God whereas all other powers apart from it are of a created nature;[3] and it is the same with all the other natural powers of God. It is thus not

93

true that the essence of God is the only unoriginate reality, and that all realities other than it are of a created nature.[4]

6

My discourse (guided by the absolute and eternally preexisting nature) now leads me briefly to show the unbelieving that not only the divine powers (which the Fathers often call "natural energies"), but also some works[5] of God are without beginning, as the Fathers also rightly affirm. For was it not needful for the work of providence to exist before Creation, so as to cause each of the created things to come to be in time, out of nonbeing? Was it not necessary for a divine knowledge to know before choosing, even outside time? But how does it follow that the divine prescience had a beginning? How could one conceive of a beginning of God's self-contemplation, and was there ever a moment when God began to be moved toward contemplation of Himself? Never!

There is, therefore, a single unoriginate providence, that of God, and it is a work of God. Providences other than it are of a created nature. Nonetheless, providence is not the divine essence, and thus the essence of God is not alone unoriginate. There is in the same way only one unoriginate and uncreated prescience, that of God, whereas presciences different from it—those which we possess by nature—all have a beginning and are created. There is also only one will without beginning, that of God, whereas all wills other than it have a beginning. However, no one would dare to say that the essence of God is a will, not even those who claimed the Word of God was a son of God's will.[6] As for predeterminations, their very name shows that they existed before creation; and should anyone wish to deny their existence before the ages, he would be refuted by Paul's words, that "God has foreordained before the ages".[7]

These works of God, then, are manifestly unoriginate and pre-temporal: His foreknowledge, will, providence, contemplation of Himself, and whatever powers are akin to these. But if this contemplation, providence, prescience, predetermination and will are works of God that are without beginning, then virtue is also unoriginate, for each of His works is a virtue;[8] existence is also unoriginate, since it precedes not only essence[9] but all beings, for it is the first existence. And are not will and predetermination virtues?

7

... The wise Maximus thus rightly says that "existence, life, holiness and virtue are works of God that do not have a beginning in time";[10] and he adds (so that no one should think these things relate to this age, albeit in a nontemporal sense), "There was never a time when virtue, goodness, holiness and immortality did not exist."[11] He then makes this further observation, lest anyone should think the virtues in us are unoriginate: "Things that have a beginning exist, and are said to exist by participation in things unoriginate. For God is the creator of all life, all immortality, all sanctity and all virtue",[12] that is, of that which subsists in us by nature.[13] ... Elsewhere, he states, "These virtues are contemplated as qualities appertaining essentially to God", and are participable.[14] Created beings participate in them, as do works of God that have an origin in time, but they themselves are works without beginning.[15] "For nonbeing is not anterior to virtue," he says, "nor to any other of the realities mentioned before, since they have God as the eternal and absolutely unique originator of their being."[16] And so that no one should believe he is speaking of the superessentiality to which our intellect attains after having stripped itself of all created things,[17] he continues, "God infinitely transcends these participable virtues an infinite number of times."[18] In other words, He infinitely transcends that goodness, holiness and virtue which are unoriginate, that is, uncreated.

Thus, neither the uncreated goodness, nor the eternal glory, nor the divine life nor things akin to these *are* simply the superessential essence of God, for God transcends them all as Cause. But we say He is life, goodness and so forth, and give Him these names, because of the revelatory energies and powers of the Superessential. As Basil the Great says, "The guarantee of the existence of every essence is its natural energy which leads the mind to the nature."[19] And according to St. Gregory of Nyssa and all the other Fathers, the natural energy is the power which manifests every essence, and only nonbeing is deprived of this power; for the being which participates in an essence will also surely participate in the power which naturally manifests that essence.

But since God is entirely present in each of the divine energies, we name Him from each of them, although it is clear that He transcends all of them. For, given the multitude of divine energies, how could God subsist entirely in each without any division at all; and how could each provide Him with a name and manifest Him entirely, thanks to indivisible and supernatural simplicity, if He did not transcend all these energies?[20]

8

There *are*, however, energies of God which have a beginning and an end, as all the saints will confirm.[21] Our opponent . . . thinks that everything which has a beginning is created; this is why he has stated that only one reality is unoriginate, the essence of God, adding that "what is not this essence, derives from a created nature."[22] But even if this man considers that everything that has a beginning is created, we for our part know that while all the energies of God are uncreated, not all are without beginning. Indeed, beginning and end must be ascribed, if not to the creative power itself, then at least to its activity, that is to say, to its energy as directed towards created things. Moses showed this, when he said, "God rested from all the works which He had begun to do."[23]

How then would the Superessential One not be different from its proper energy? But, he asks, are the unoriginate energies identical with the Superessential One? There are among them some which have an end but not a beginning, as Basil the Great has said concerning the prescience of God.[24] The superessential essence of God is thus not to be identified with the energies, even with those without beginning; from which it follows that it is not only transcendent to any energy whatsoever, but that it transcends them "to an infinite degree and an infinite number of times", as the divine Maximus says.[25]

9

The blessed Cyril, for his part, says that the divine energy and power consist in the fact that God is everywhere and contains all, without being contained by anything.[26] But it does not follow that the Divine *Nature* consists in the fact of being everywhere, any more than our own nature uniquely consists in being somewhere. For how could our essence consist in a fact which is in no way an essence? Essence and energy are thus not totally identical in God, even though He is entirely manifest in every energy, His essence being indivisible.

John Chrysostom, on the other hand, says that the essential energy of God consists in being nowhere; not in the sense that it does not exist, but in the sense that it transcends place, time and nature.[27] . . . As Basil the Great asks, "Is it not ridiculous to say that the creative power is an essence, and similarly, that providence is an essence, and foreknowledge, simply taking every energy as essence?"[28] And the divine Maximus says, "Goodness and all that the word implies, all life absolutely, all immortality, and all the attributes that appertain essentially to God are works of God, and do not have a temporal beginning. Nonbeing, that is to say, is not anterior to virtue, nor to any of the realities mentioned above, even though the beings which participate in them began to exist in time."[29] None of these things is the essence of God—neither the uncreated goodness, nor the unoriginate eternal life; all these exist not in Him, but around Him.[30]

10

Moreover, the Holy Fathers affirm unanimously that it is impossible to find a name to manifest the nature of the uncreated Trinity, but that the names belong to the energies. "The divinity" also designates an energy, that of moving or contemplating or burning,[31] or else it indicates the "deification-in-itself."[32] But He Who is beyond every name is not identical with what He is named; for the essence and energy of God are not identical. But if the divinity of God designates the divine energy *par excellence*, and if the energies are, as you say, created, the divinity of God must also be created!

However, it is not only uncreated, but unoriginate; for He Who knows all things before their creation did not begin to contemplate created beings in time. But the divine essence that transcends all names, also surpasses energy, to the extent that the subject of an action surpasses its object; and He Who is beyond every name transcends what is named according to the same measure. But this is in no way opposed to the veneration of a unique God and a unique divinity, since the fact of calling the ray "sun" in no way prevents us from thinking of a unique sun and a unique light. Do you not see how strictly our views accord with those of the saints?[33]

11

But as for you, you allege all that is participable is created, that not only the works, but also the powers and energies of God have a beginning and a temporal end! . . . You accuse of impiety and threaten with excommunication and anathema those saints who glorify God according to His essence, which exceeds even His uncreated energies, since this essence transcends all affirmation and all negation. Since you hold and teach these opinions, have you any way of proving that you are not to be classed with the heretics of past times, since you declare that not only are all the energies and all the works of God created, but even the very powers of this superessential nature?

Indeed, even this name "essence" designates one of the powers in God. Denys the Areopagite says, "If we call the superessential Mystery 'God' or 'Life' or 'Essence' or 'Light' or 'Word', we are referring to nothing other than the deifying powers which proceed from God and come down to us, creating substance, giving life, and granting wisdom."[34] So, when you say that only the essence of God is an unoriginate reality, you give us to understand that only one power of God is without beginning, that which creates substance, whereas all the others apart from this one are temporal.[35]

Yet why should the substance-creating power be unoriginate, when (according to you) the vivifying power has a temporal beginning, as also the life-giving and wisdom-bestowing powers? Either all the divine powers are unoriginate, or none! If you say that only one of them is uncreated, you expel the others from the realm of the uncreated; and if you declare all are created, you must also reject this single uncreated one. For such a falsehood is self-contradictory and inconsistent with itself! . . .

12

Perhaps he will say that it is "through the essence" that God is said to possess all these powers in Himself in a unique and unifying manner. But, in the first place, it would be necessary to call this reality "God", for such is the term for it which we have received from the Church. When God was conversing with Moses, He did not say, "I am the essence", but "I am the One Who is."[36] Thus it is not the One Who is who derives from the essence, but essence which derives from Him, for it is He who contains all being in Himself.[37]

So if, instead of speaking of "essence", he had employed the word "God", he would also have had to say "by nature"—and this by reason of grace and the "gods by grace",[38] whom the saints say are "unoriginate and uncreated by grace", when speaking on this subject.[39] Thus he should have said, "There is one God, unoriginate *by nature.*" But he has replaced the word "God" by another, and omitted "by nature", so as to mislead his hearers as far as possible, and has not said that the only reality without beginning is He Who holds all things together and unifies all, yet preexists all. If this had been his meaning, why would he have made so much effort to show that the natural powers in God are created?

13

To convince you that this man believes the divine powers to be created, listen to his own words, which are perfectly clear. He brings forward the words of the great Denys: "The providential powers produced by the imparticipable God are Being-in-itself, Life-in-itself and Divinity-in-itself; to the extent to which created beings participate in them according to their proper mode, we can say that they *are* living and divine beings, and thus it can be said that the Good One has established them."[40]

This is what Barlaam concludes from this: "The Divinity-in-itself and the other realities which the great Denys has here clearly called powers, are not eternal, but the Good One has also granted existence to them." And again: "A certain Father[41] has said that there is a thearchy and a divinity transcended by the Principle of the universe, but he did not say that they were eternal, since the universal Cause gave them also existence." And also: "There is a glory of God beyond participation, an eternal reality, and thus identical to the divine essence; and there is a participable glory, different from this essence and not eternal, for the universal Cause has given it existence."[42]

As I said above, he who said that the angels contemplate the eternal glory—I mean St. Gregory Nazianzen[43]—has shown that it is an error to identify the eternal glory of God with the imparticipable essence of God. We have here a proof that the eternal glory of God *is* participable, for that which in God is visible in some way, is also participable.[44] But the great Denys has also said: "The divine intelligences move in a circular movement, united to the unoriginate and endless rays of the Beautiful and Good."[45] It is clear, therefore, that these unoriginate and endless rays are other than the imparticipable essence of God, and different (albeit inseparable) from the essence.

In the first place, that essence is one, even though the rays are many, and are sent out in a manner appropriate to those participating in them, being multiplied according to the varying capacity of those receiving them.[46] This is what Paul means when he speaks of "the parts of the Holy Spirit".[47] Furthermore, the essence is superessential, and I believe no one would deny that these rays are its energies or energy, and that one may participate in them, even though the essence remains beyond participation.

14

Moreover, every union is through contact, sensible in the realm of sense perception, intellectual in that of intellect. And since there is union with these illuminations, there must be contact with them, of an intellectual, or rather a spiritual, kind. As for the divine essence, that is in itself beyond all contact.

Now, this union with the illuminations—what is it, if not a vision? The rays are consequently visible to those worthy, although the divine essence is absolutely invisible, and these unoriginate and endless rays are a light without beginning or end. There exists, then, an eternal light, other than the divine essence; it is not itself an essence—far from it!—but an energy of the Superessential. This light without beginning or end is neither sensible nor intelligible, in the proper sense. It is spiritual and divine, distinct from all creatures in its transcendence; and what is neither sensible nor intelligible does not fall within the scope of the senses as such, nor of the intellectual faculty considered in itself.[48]

This spiritual light is thus not only the object of vision, but it is also the power by which we see; it is neither a sensation nor an intellection, but is a spiritual power, distinct from all created cognitive faculties in its transcendence, and made present by grace in rational natures which have been purified.

15

For this reason, Gregory the Theologian not only said that the good angels "contemplate an eternal glory",[49] but that they contemplate it "eternally", showing that it is not a created, natural and intellectual faculty which allows the angels to contemplate the eternal glory of God, but an eternal power, spiritual and divine. "It is not in order that God should be glorified," he says, "for one can add nothing to the Fullness and to the Giver of good things to others; but so that the first natures after God should never cease to receive His benefits."[50]

Do you not see that the angels do not naturally possess the eternal vision of the eternal glory, but they receive this power and contemplation as a free gift from the Eternal Nature, as do the saints?[51]

According to Basil the Great, "That which is set in motion by the Holy Spirit becomes an eternal movement, living and holy; when the Spirit comes to dwell in a man, he who was previously only earth and dust receives the dignity of a prophet, an apostle, and an angel of God."[52] It is by such a power that the heavenly intelligences are said to see: Thus that light is accessible to the intellect and yet transcends it. It is also said of them that they see themselves; for that light is visible by virtue of itself: Inaccessible to the created cognitive faculty, this power is contemplated by those deemed worthy.

16

This is why the great Denys has said that "the intelligences follow a circular motion, for they are united to the unoriginate and endless illuminations."[53] One should note that this Father, who always speaks with the greatest precision, did not say simply that the intelligences follow a circular motion . . . but that they "are told" to follow this motion—meaning by this, in my opinion, that this motion is not natural to them, even though from the beginning they are co-heirs of grace, having never experienced pollution.[54]

On the other hand, their greatest enemy[55] can also provide evidence, most worthy of belief, that this light and power of vision does not inhere by nature in the supracosmic angels. The race of demons, which has fallen away from them, has been deprived of the light and power of vision, but not of those faculties natural to it. This light and vision are thus not natural to the angels.[56] The demonic race has certainly not been deprived of intellection, for the demons are intelligences and have not lost their being. They say, "I know who you are, the Holy One of God";[57] and He did not permit them to say "that they knew He was the Christ."[58] This is why Gregory the Theologian remarked, "You do not believe in the Divinity? Even the demons believe in it."[59] And if they know the divinity, they necessarily know that it is not to be identified with any created thing.

17

This light, then, is not a knowledge, neither does one acquire it by any affirmation or negation. Each evil angel is an intelligence, but, as the prophets say, an "Assyrian" intelligence,[60] which makes a bad use of knowledge. Indeed, it is impossible to make a bad use of *this* light, for it instantly quits anyone who leans towards evil, and leaves bereft of God any man who gives himself over to depravity.[61]

This light and this knowledge, then, are not, strictly speaking, an intellection, even though one may in a loose sense use such a term, for it is mind above all that receives them; just as one may call them "Divinity" because of Him who mysteriously energises this grace. For it is a divinising energy which is in no way separate from the energising Spirit.[62] The man illuminated by purity has a beginning, in that he has received illumination—the Fathers for this reason call it "purity"—but the light and the illumination have no beginning. We see this particularly in the case of those men who have been illuminated in the manner of the angels, and have received deification; as Maximus says, "Contemplating the light of the invisible and more-than-ineffable glory, they themselves also receive the blessed purity, together with the powers on high."

18

And if we look for the reason why this innovator has been led to imagine that the deifying grace of the Spirit (or rather, all the powers of God) are created, then apart from that wretched source of heresy, mentioned by us above,[63] the only reason is the statement by Denys, that God has *established* these powers.[64]

But this word refers only to their existence, not to their mode of existence. One could thus apply it to those beings which proceed from God, whether created or uncreated. Indeed, Basil the Great used this term of the Son, when he said, "He who made the waterfloods,[65] did He not establish the Son, just as He did these waters?"[66] And, speaking of the Holy Spirit, he said: "He is the Spirit of the mouth of God,[67] so that you should not take Him for an object deriving from outside God and so place Him among the creatures, but should consider that He has His hypostasis from God."[68] And again: "This is the mark of His hypostatic individuation—to be made known through the Son, and to be established from the Father."[69] Gregory the Theologian likewise often calls the generation of the Son before the ages an "hypostasis" (or "establishment").[70]

So you may just as well demonstrate on the basis of such terminology that the Son and Holy Spirit are creatures, since the only reason that leads you to declare that the divine powers are created rests on the fact that the universal Cause has also "established" them.[71] You have failed to notice that the great Denys has shown here that these powers are said not to exist by reason of their transcendence; for in speaking of the "providential powers sent by the God beyond participation", he adds, "The created beings which participate in them are called 'beings', in the sense that these powers transcend all that is."[72] And Maximus, while stating that the participating beings have a beginning, affirms that that in which they participate has no beginning.[73]

III. iii. 5

"Is it true," Barlaam asks, "that a man sees God when he elevates himself above mankind? For then he would become an angel! But the best of our theologians is inferior to the least of the angels; and even if we admitted he became an angel, it is nonetheless the case that they do not see the essence of God."

... If the emperor wished to do a soldier the honour of speaking to him personally, the soldier would not immediately become a general; even though this soldier was at this moment the person nearest to the emperor, he would not for all that assume the dignity of a general.[74] "But," he says, "a man can only meet God through the mediation of an angel, for we are subordinate to the angelic hierarchy." What are you saying? Are you trying to make subject to necessity Him Who is Master of necessity, and Who suppresses these requirements when He wishes, and sometimes transforms them entirely?[75]

Tell me, which of the angels was it that said to Moses, "I am He who is, the God of Abraham, Isaac and Jacob,"[76] if not the Son of God, as the great Basil has written?[77] What do these words of Exodus signify: "The Lord spoke to Moses face to face, as a man speaks to his friend"?[78] And if He Who spoke to Abraham and "swore by Himself"[79] was only an angel, how could the Apostle have said, "He could not swear by one greater than Himself"?[80] But if God saw fit to speak Himself to those Fathers in the shadow of the Law, how much the more has He manifested Himself directly to the saints, now that the truth has appeared, and the law of grace has been shown forth! According to this law of grace, it is the Lord Himself who has saved us, "not an angel or a man,"[81] and the very Spirit of God who has instructed us in all truth. Was He not pleased to become man to save us?[82] Has He not borne the Cross and death for our sake, even though "we were still unrighteous,"[83] as the Apostle says? Did He not deign to make His dwelling in man, to appear to him and speak to him without intermediary, so that man should be not only righteous, but sanctified and purified in advance in soul and body by keeping the divine commandments, and so be transformed into a vehicle worthy to receive the all-powerful Spirit? It is on this that Gregory of Nyssa insists, when, having called to mind the celestial and supernatural vision of Stephen, he asks, "Was this an achievement of human nature? Was it an angel who so exalted the nature which lay prostrate here below? No—for it is not written that Stephen possessed exceptional qualities, or that he was surrounded with angelic assistance when he saw what he did; but that Stephen, full of the Holy Spirit, saw the glory of God and the only Son of God.[84] For (as the prophet says)[85] it is not possible to see the light without seeing *in* the light."[86] Gregory of Nyssa is here talking of a vision accessible through the Spirit, not of a form of cognition; it is to this latter sense of "knowledge" that he applies the expression, "No one has seen God",[87] and by opposing to this the spiritual contemplation of Stephen, he has provided us with the best and most orthodox solution. In addition, he did not say that the divine essence was accessible and visible, but only that this was the case with the glory of the Father and the grace of the Spirit.[88]

6

"But," Barlaam says, "I have heard that this grace and glory are supernatural and akin to God, for it is said that like is contemplated by like.[89] So, since this reality is uncreated and unoriginate, I say that it is the essence of God."[90] But this is impossible! ... Is the divine energy neither supernatural nor unoriginate nor uncreated nor like to God, even though it manifests God in His entirety through itself to those who contemplate in a supernatural manner in the Spirit?

"Only the essence of God is uncreated and unoriginate", he says, "but every energy is created." What impiety! It follows from this that God has no natural and essential energies. This amounts to openly denying the existence of God—for the saints clearly state, in conformity with St. Maximus,[91] that no nature can exist or be known, unless it possesses an essential energy. Alternatively, it follows that there are divine energies, but that these, although natural and essential, are yet created; and in consequence, the essence of God which possesses them is itself created. For the essence and the nature whose natural and essential energies are created is itself created and made known as such.[92]

7

Tell me: How would we come to know Christ in two energies and two natures, if the natural energies of God are not uncreated? How would we know Him in the two wills, if He did not possess as God a natural and a divine will? And what is the will of God, if not an energy of the divine nature?[93] Is the will of the Uncreated then created? Is He subject to time and to a beginning, and did He acquire a will which He did not possess before the ages? How did He acquire it—by necessity or by a change of opinion? With these novelties, this unfortunate man defames not only the divine nature but also the incarnation of the Saviour; having decided to attack Christianity, he expels himself from the orthodox community of Christians, and provides proof in his treatises that he is nothing but a Monophysite and a Monothelite, worse than those who appeared in earlier times![94]

In fact, according to you, every divine energy, apart from the essence of God which is the prime mover of the universe, has a beginning in time. Consequently, every divine energy is necessarily created; and Christ did not possess in accord with His two natures energies both created and uncreated, but only created energies. He had, then, only a single energy, which was not even divine (as the ancient heretics used to say) but all His energies derived from the created order. And if He had only one energy, He necessarily had only one nature which also was not divine but created, as the Monophysites once held, for the nature whose energy is created is not itself uncreated.

8

For if God did not possess unoriginate energies—but transcended them, to the extent that the agent is superior to his action—how could He be anterior and superior to that which is unoriginate? Similarly, He would not be "more-than-God", as St. Denys puts it, if "the reality of the deifying gift" were not called "divinity"[95]—a reality which, according to St. Maximus, "eternally exists from the eternal God".[96] If it is not so, deified man would participate in the *nature* of God, and be God by nature.[97]

Thus, just as God would not be called "more-than-God" if the grace of deification did not exist, so He would not be called "more-than-unoriginate", unless, as St. Maximus has rightly said, "immortality, infinity, being and all those realities which by nature are contemplated as qualities appertaining to God are the unoriginate works of God".[98]

If grace were not unoriginate, how would one become through participation in this grace "unoriginate like Melchisedec, of whom it is said that his days had no beginning and his life no end"?[99] Or how, "like Paul, could a man live the divine and eternal life of the Word dwelling in him"?[100]

9

"But even if we grant that the divine energies are uncreated," he says, "it is still the case that no one has seen them, unless they have become created." ... But they never became created, since only those things that participate in them are created, whereas the energies in which those things participate[101] preexist in God. Otherwise, the creatures would participate in the divine essence, which is the greatest absurdity. But let us set this issue aside now.

We do not see distant objects as if they were in front of our eyes, nor the future as if it were the present; we do not know the will of God concerning us before it comes to be. Yet the prophets knew the designs of God which eternally preexisted in God, even before they were accomplished. Similarly, the chosen disciples saw the essential and eternal beauty of God on Thabor (as the Church sings)[102] ... not the glory of God which derives from creatures, as you think, but the superluminous splendour of the beauty of the Archetype;[103] the very formless form of the divine loveliness, which deifies man and makes him worthy of personal converse with God; the very Kingdom of God, eternal and endless, the very light beyond intellection and unapproachable, the heavenly and infinite light, out of time and eternal, the light that makes immortality shine forth, the light which deifies those who contemplate it. They indeed saw the same grace of the Spirit which would later dwell in them;[104] for there is only one grace of the Father, Son and Spirit, and they saw it with their corporeal eyes, but with eyes that had been opened so that, instead of being blind, they could see[105]—as St. John of Damascus puts it,[106] they contemplated that uncreated light which, even in the age to come, will be ceaselessly visible only to the saints, as Sts. Denys[107] and Maximus teach.

10

Do you not see that these divine energies are *in* God, and remain invisible to the created faculties? Yet the saints see them, because they have transcended themselves with the help of the Spirit. As we read: "He who has been found worthy to enter into God will perceive pre-existing in God all those inner principles of created things, through a simple and indivisible knowledge."[108] And again: "There will no longer be any reason for the thinking soul to be divided into many parts, because it will be recollected in itself and in God. For its head will then be crowned by the Word of God, the first, the one and unique, in whom in a unifying manner all the causes of things are pre-established in a single incomprehensible simplicity. When such a soul fixes its gaze on the Word—Who will not be exterior to it, but entirely united to it in its simplicity—it will itself know the inner principles of things; and thanks to this knowledge, will perhaps allow itself to use the methods of distinction, before entering into nuptial union with the divine Word."[109]

Do you not understand that the men who are united to God and deified, who fix their eyes in a divine manner on Him, do not see as we do? Miraculously, they see with a sense that exceeds the senses, and with a mind that exceeds mind,[110] for the power of the spirit penetrates their human faculties, and allows them to see things which are beyond us. In speaking of a vision through the senses, then, we must add that this transcends the senses, in order to show clearly that it is not only supernatural, but goes beyond all expression.

Yet this quibbler . . . accuses us falsely of regarding God as sensible reality.[111] It is as if someone were to separate the essence from the Superessential, on the pretext that God is called "superessential essence". He is not ashamed to maintain the following: "Since you say that God possesses an essence, it follows either that God is a generic idea, contemplated merely in abstract thought, and not possessing real existence, or else that He is a particular object." . . . When we speak of a spiritual and superintelligible reality, you take this to mean that it is accessible to the senses. You fail to understand that God's inner being is not at all the same as an existent object, and you imagine wrongly that the things around God—the natural attributes appertaining to Him—are identical with His inner being.[112]

11

"But," he continues, "God would be no different from visible things, if one could see Him according to that which surrounds Him. For each visible thing is visible, not in its inner being, but according to what surrounds it: It is not the essence of the sun which the eye perceives, but that which surrounds the essence."[113]

First, the example you bring forward shows that you purposely vilify God and His saints. For one applies the word "sun" to the rays as well as to the source of the rays; yet it does not follow that there are two suns. There is, then, a single God, even though one says that the deifying grace is *from* God. The light is also one of the things that "surround" the sun, yet it is certainly not the essence of the sun. So how could the light which shines from God upon the saints be the essence of God? Does the light of the sun appear only when one sees it, or does it exist before one has seen it? Much more so is this the case with the light which deifies those who contemplate it.

For if God in no way differed in this respect from any visible object, why is it not seen either by you or by those who think as you do, or by those who are better men than you? If only your eyes, blind as they are to this light that the saints behold . . . would teach you that it is not a natural light, nor visible though the medium of air![114] In this way, you would avoid insulting the Age to Come, for those who speak in God teach clearly that *then* we will have no need of either air or the light that passes through the air.[115] Yet you nonetheless claim that this light which is inaccessible to the power of the senses, this beauty of the eternal Age to Come, is sensible, and that then[116] too, it will be visible through the air.

12

"But if I am incapable of seeing this light," he says, "I have still my ears with which to hear the words, 'God can be dimly grasped by the mind alone from the attributes which surround Him, and He illuminates the directive faculty of the soul only when we are purified, like a lightning flash suddenly glimpsed and then swiftly passing away.' "[117] . . . Yet what does the Theologian say further on? "This is why God begins by illuminating the mind alone with an obscure light, so as to draw a man to Himself by that within Himself which is comprehensible, and so as to evoke his wonder at that which is incomprehensible, and through this wonder to increase his longing, and through this longing to purify him."[118]

What is purified by this longing? The mind alone? No—for, according to the Fathers, it does not need to make a great effort in order to be purified, and at the same time by nature it easily falls away from purity. This is why it can be purified without the desire for God, as this theologian has shown, and such a purification is appropriate for beginners. As for the desire for God, by purifying all the faculties and powers of the soul and body, and by gaining for the mind a purification that endures, it makes man receptive to deifying grace.[119]

"This is why the Divine One purifies the man who desires Him: by this purification, He creates men of divine character, conversing as with friends with those who have attained this state; and (to use a daring expression) uniting Himself as God with gods, and making Himself known to them perhaps to the same extent that He knows those who are known to Him."[120] This is something far beyond the "dim illumination" of which Barlaam speaks. Gregory is saying that they know God as well as God knows them. How? Not by the feeble efforts of the reason, of which Barlaam was speaking at the start of this chapter; but by virtue of the fact that they know God in God, that they are united to Him and so have already acquired the form of God. So they lay hold of the most divine graces of the Spirit by a divine power—graces upon which those men cannot look who do not have this divine likeness, and who seek the things around God by mind alone.

13

It is already clear that knowledge of God by experience comes from the grace that grants man the likeness of God. But how do we know that this grace is also light? ... The divine Maximus, after speaking of the union with the mystery of divine simplicity, which awaits the saints in the Age to Come, concludes: "So, beholding the light of the hidden and more-than-ineffable glory, in company with the celestial powers, they become themselves capable of receiving the blessed purity."[121]

How then do we know this light is also deification? Listen to the same Father. Having explained as far as possible the way in which deified men are united to God—a union akin to that of the soul and the body, so that the whole man should be entirely deified, divinised by the grace of the incarnate God—he concludes: "He remains entirely man by nature in his soul and body, and becomes entirely God in his soul and body through grace, and through the divine radiance of the blessed glory with which he is made entirely resplendent."[122] Do you note that this light is the radiance of God? Is the radiance of God then created?

But hear what follows: "One can never imagine anything more luminous and more sublime; for what more could those deemed worthy of deification desire?"[123] Did you not hear that this radiance is deification, and that for those made worthy, nothing is more sublime? But learn that this radiance is also the bond by which God is united to those worthy: "By it God, Who is united to those who have become gods, makes all things His own by His goodness."[124] This, then, is the deifying gift which Denys the Areopagite ... calls "divinity", while affirming that God transcends this gift.[125] What then becomes of your "knowledge", your "imitation", your "negation", with which you seek to strip the multitude of the knowledge which comes from faith and the true imitation of God which transcends us?

14

"But," Barlaam says, "even if Denys said that God exceeds this 'divinity', he did not say that God exceeds even nonbeing by reason of His transcendence." ... When Denys said that "God possesses the superessential in a superessential manner",[126] what else does he affirm except precisely this? Since that which is nonbeing by virtue of transcendence *is* superessential,[127] God is even beyond that, for He possesses the superessential superessentially.

But how do you regard the man, or rather men—for they are one, as the Master prayed that they might be one,[128] and when we refer to one, we mean all the saints—how then do you regard the men who speak of a God infinitely transcendent to all the deification imparted from His superessential nature? How will you reply to one who affirms that the divine transcendence is beyond all affirmation and all negation?[129] Is He not beyond nonbeing in His transcendence? It is also said that God is beyond uncreated immortality, life and goodness—yet, unable to fix your gaze on the summits of such sound theology ... you have rejected all the Fathers. But they ... tell us that God transcends all else "an infinite number of times",[130] since they know that His transcendence is inexpressible by any thought or word whatsoever. But enough on this subject.

15

We must also briefly show that our opponent has transformed virtue into vice, for he calls "impassibility" the state in which the passionate part of the soul finds itself in a state of death: "The activity of this passionate part of the soul," he says, "completely blinds and gouges out the divine eye, and so does not allow any of its faculties to come into play."[131] Alas! Should hatred of evil and love of God and neighbour gouge out the divine eye? Yet these are activities of the passionate part of the soul. Indeed, it is with this faculty of the soul that we love or else turn away, that we unite ourselves or else remain strangers. Those who love the good thus transform this power, and do not put it to death; they do not enclose it immovable in themselves, but activate it towards love of God and their neighbours—for, according to the Lord's words, "on these two commands hang all the Law and the Prophets."[132]

Notes

Preface

1. See my *The Spirit of Eastern Christendom (1600–1700)*, Volume 2 of *The Christian Tradition* (Chicago, 1974), pp. 254–70.

2. Martin Jugie, "Palamas Grégoire," *Dictionnaire de théologie catholique* (15 vols.; Paris, 1903–50), XI-2:1735–1776; and "Palamite (Controverse)," *ibid.*, 1777–1818.

3. Adrian Fortescue, "Hesychasm," *The Catholic Encyclopedia* (15 vols.; New York, 1903), VII:301–3. See also the long article "Greek Church," *ibid.*, VI:752–72, by Siméon Vailhé, whose discussion of Palamas speaks of his "monstrous errors" and concludes with the remarkable sentence: "Thirty years of incessant controversy and discordant councils ended with a resurrection of polytheism."

4. Daniel Honorius Hunter, "Palamas, Gregory," *New Catholic Encyclopedia* (15 vols.; New York, 1967), X:872–74.

5. *The Documents of Vatican II*, edited by Walter M. Abbott (New York, 1966), p. 373.

6. See the comments of Alexander Schemann, *ibid.*, pp. 387–88.

7. John Meyendorff, *St. Gregory Palamas and Orthodox Spirituality*, translated by Adele Fiske (Tuckahoe, 1974), pp. 119–29.

8. Etienne Gilson, *God and Philosophy* (New Haven, 1941), p. 41.

9. Irénée Hausherr, "La méthode d'oraison hésychaste," *Orientalia Christiana*, IX (1927): 1–210.

10. Nicolas Zernov, *The Russian Religious Renaissance of the Twentieth Century* (New York, 1963), esp. pp. 250–82.

11. Simon Karlinsky, "Foreword" to *The Bitter Air of Exile: Russian Writers in the West 1922–1972*, edited by Simon Karlinsky and Alfred Appel, Jr. (Berkeley, 1977), p. 6.

NOTES

12. See my brief essay, *"Puti Russkogo Bogoslova:* When Orthodoxy Comes West," *The Heritage of the Early Church: Essays in Honor of the Very Reverend Georges Vasilievich Florovsky* (Rome, 1973), pp. 11–16.

13. Vladimir Lossky, *In the Image and Likeness of God,* edited by John H. Erickson and Thomas E. Bird (Tuckahoe, 1974), pp. 45–69.

Introduction

1. *Rer. mon.,* Migne, PG 40, col. 1253B.

2. *In inscr. psalm.,* Migne, PG 44, col. 456C; ed. W. Jaeger (Leiden, 1962), p. 44.

3. Justinian, *Nov.* 5, 3; ed. R. Schoell and G. Kroll, p. 32.

4. Evagrius, *The Praktikos. Chapters on Prayer,* tr. J. E. Bamberger (Spencer, Mass.: Cistercian Publications, 1970), pp. 63, 69.

5. On Evagrius and his influence, see particularly I. Hausherr, "L'hésychasme, étude de spiritualité", in *Orientalia Christiana Periodica* 22 (1956): 5–40 (with reference to earlier and important studies by the same author).

6. On this, see particularly A. Guillaumont, *Les Kephalaia Gnostica d'Evagre le Pontique et l'histoire de l'origénisme chez les Syriens* (Paris, 1962).

7. On the role of the heart in early Christian spirituality, see particularly A. Guillaumont, "Le Coeur chez les spirituels grecs à l'époque ancienne", in the article "Cor et cordis affectus", in *Dictionnaire de spiritualité* 14, 15 (Paris, 1952), cols. 2281–2288.

8. *Hom.* 15, 20, Migne, PG 34, col. 589AB; ed. H. Dörries (Berlin, 1964), p. 139.

9. On the Messalian interpretation of Macarius, see particularly H. Dörries, *Die Überlieferung des messalianischen Makarius-Schriften* (Leipzig, 1941); for a different view, J. Meyendorff, "Messalianism or anti-Messalianism? A Fresh Look at the Macarian Problem", in *Kyriakon. Festschrift Johannes Quasten,* ed. P. Granfield and J. J. Jungmann (Münster Westf., 1974), pp. 585–590.

10. The most famous and influential collection of writings concerned with the hesychast prayer tradition is the *Philokalia* published by St. Nicodemus the Haghiorite in 1782. The publication of a full English translation is in progress, *The Philokalia* 1, tr. and ed. G. E. H. Palmer, P. Sherrard, and K. Ware (London: Faber and Faber, 1979). For a short survey of the hesychast tradition before Palamas, see J. Meyendorff, *St. Gregory Palamas and Orthodox Spirituality* (Crestwood, N.Y.: St. Vladimir's Seminary Press, 1974), pp. 7–71.

11. The biography of Gregory Palamas is known to us primarily through an *Encomion* composed by his friend and disciple, Philotheos Kokkinos, Patriarch of Constantinople, text in Migne, PG 151, cols. 551–656. For a complete account, see J. Meyendorff, *A Study of Gregory Palamas* (London and New

NOTES

York: Faith Press and St. Vladimir's Seminary Press, 2nd ed., 1974), pp. 28–113.

12. On this episode, the most recent study is A. Philippidis-Brat, "La captivité de Palamas chez les Turcs: dossier et commentaire", *Travaux et mémoires, Centre de recherche d'histoire et civilisation byzantines 7* (Paris, 1979), pp. 109–221.

13. Cf. an attempt to date the death of Palamas as early as 1357 in H. V. Beyer, "Eine Chronologie der Lebensgeschichte des Nikophoros Gregoras", *Jahrbuch der Österreichischen Byzantinistik* 27 (Band, Wien, 1978) pp. 150–153. However, the argument for 1359 based on the very precise data given by the *Encomion* of Philotheos (Palamas died at 63 after twelve and a half years as bishop) carries more weight.

14. Ed. J. Meyendorff, *Grégoire Palamas. Défense des saints hesychastes. Introduction, Texte critique, traduction et notes* (Louvain, 2nd ed., 1973), I, pp. I–L; cf. also the series of my earlier studies reprinted in *Byzantine Hesychasm: Historical, Theological and Social Problems* (London: Variorum Reprints, 1974) and an updated chronology in R. E. Sinkewicz "A new interpretation for the first episode in the controversy between Barlaam the Calabrian and Gregory Palamas," *The Journal of Theological Studies*, xxxi, 2, 1980, 489–500.

15. The complete edition of the theological writings of Palamas is in the process of completion by P. Chrestou (cf. *Palama Syngrammata*, Thessaloniki, vol. 1, 1962; vol. 2, 1966; vol. 3, 1970). In references below, the title of this edition is abbrieviated as P.S.

16. There is abundant recent publication on this subject by authors adopting different and sometimes contradictory points of view; see, for example, I. P. Medvedev, *Vizantiisky Gumanizm* 14–15, 20 (Leningrad, 1976); G. Podskalsky, *Theologie und Philosophie in Byzanz* (München, 1977); R. E. Sinkewicz, "The doctrine of the knowledge of God in the early writings of Barlaam the Calabrian" *Mediaeval Studies* XLIV, 1982, 181–242. For a general objective and accessible presentation, see particularly D. M. Nicol, *Church and Society in the Last Centuries of Byzantium. The Birkbeck Lectures, 1977* (New York: Cambridge University Press, 1979).

17. J. Gouillard, "Le Synodikon de l'Orthodoxie. Edition et commentaire", *Centre de recherche d'histoire et de civilisation byzantines. Travaux et mémoires 2* (Paris, 1967), p. 59; also Triodion (Athens, ed. Phos, 1958), p. 160.

18. *First letter to Palamas*, ed. G. Schirò, in *Barlaam Calabro epistole greche i primordi episodici e dottrinari delle lotte esicaste* (Palermo, 1954), p. 262.

19. *Tr.* I, 1, 20, tr. below, p. 28.

20. *Tr.* I, 1, quest., tr. below, p. 25.

21. See, for example, *Tr.* I, 1, 14–15; I, 1, 13; etc.; see below, p. 27.

22. Some art historians have attempted to connect the victory of Palamism with a decay of the so-called Palaeologan Renaissance in Byzantine art.

NOTES

However, the very concept of "Renaissance," when applied to Byzantine society, can have only a very relative significance. Social and cultural rather than theological factors should be used to explain its "decay" (see J. Meyendorff, "Spiritual Trends in Byzantium in the late Thirteenth and early Fourteenth Centuries," in P. Underwood, *The Kariye Djami* 4 (Princeton, N.J., 1975), pp. 93–106; also *Byzantium and the Rise of Russia* (New York, Cambridge University Press, 1981), pp. 138–144.

23. On the positions of St. Maximus on this point, see particularly L. Thunberg, *Microcosm and Mediator. The Theological Anthropology of Maximus the Confessor* (Lund, 1965) pp. 327–330.

24. Cf. my analysis of Barlaam's thought in "Un mauvais théologien de l'unité", in *L'Eglise et les églises* 2 (Chévetogne, 1955), pp. 47–64 (reprinted in *Byzantine Hesychasm* [London: Variorum, 1974]); for a more positive evaluation of Barlaam, see G. Podskalsky, *Theologie und Philosophie in Byzanz* (München, 1977), pp. 124–157.

25. V. Lossky, *The Mystical Theology of the Eastern Church* (New York, 1976), p. 43.

26. Evagrius Ponticus, Chapters on Prayer 119, tr. J. E. Bamberger, *Evagrius Ponticus. The Praktikos* (Spencer, Mass., 1970), p. 75.

27. *Tr.* I, 2, 12 and II 2, 2; ed. J. Meyendorff, pp. 99, 320–324.

28. Published by I. Hausherr in "La Méthode d'oraison hésychaste", *Orientalia Christiana Periodica* 9, 2 (1927).

29. Migne, PG 147, cols. 945–966.

30. Tr. in J. Meyendorff, *St. Gregory Palamas and Orthodox Spirituality* (Crestwood, N.Y.; St. Vladimir's Seminary Press, 1974), pp. 59–60.

31. *Ad Adelphium* 4, Migne, PG 26, col. 1077A.

32. *Chapters on Love* 3, 25, Migne, PG 90, col. 1024BC.

33. Cf., for example, *Adv. Haer.* 5, 6, 1.

34. More references and discussion in J. Meyendorff, *Byzantine Theology. Historical Trends and Doctrinal Themes* (New York: 2nd ed., 1979), pp. 138–150.

35. For the principles and terminology of post-Chalcedonian Christology, see J. Meyendorff, *Christ in Eastern Christian Thought* (New York: St. Vladimir's Seminary Press, 1975), particularly the chapter on St. Maximus, pp. 131–151.

36. *Tr.* I, 3, 38, ed. J. Meyendorff, p. 193; cf. tr. and commentary in *A Study of Gregory Palamas*, pp. 150ff.

37. This theme is particularly emphasized in the *Hagioreitic Tome*, or "Tome of the Holy Mountain", a document drafted by Palamas and signed in 1340 by representatives of the monasteries of Mount Athos in support of his theology (text in Migne, PG 150, col. 1225–1236; cf. J. Meyendorff, *A Study of Gregory Palamas*, pp. 48–49, 193–196).

38. Earlier in this century, the distinction was fiercely criticized by

116

NOTES

French Assumptionists S. Guichardan and M. Jugie, primarily in the name of the notion of simplicity of God, as defined in Latin scholastic thought. For my own presentation of the issue, see *A Study of Gregory Palamas*, pp. 202–227. For the abundant bibliography that has appeared since then, see D. Stiernon, "Bulletin sur le palamisme", *Revue des études byzantines* 30 (1972): 231–337. But the debate continues; see, for example, A. de Halleux, "Palamisme et Tradition", *Irénikon* 4 (1975): 479–493.

39. See J. Meyendorff, "Notes sur l'influence dionysienne en Orient", in *Studia patristica. Texte und Untersuchungen 64* (Berlin, 1957), pp. 547–552.

A. Philosophy does not save

1. The "I" of the questions is meant to be the bewildered disciple who appeals to Palamas for guidance in face of the attack on the monks made by Barlaam and his supporters.

2. *Apatheia:* freedom from the tyranny of the passions: an interior liberation that is the goal of monastic *ascesis.* It involves a state of stability in the virtues (*not* insensibility), in which one is no longer dominated by such impulses as anger, lust and fear, but has acquired the inner peace that frees one to love.

3. *Paideia:* Education as a process of initiation into the culture of classical antiquity. For a Byzantine Greek, it would involve an understanding of such things as grammar, rhetoric, astronomy, and above all philosophy, especially that of Plato, Aristotle and the Neoplatonists.

According to Palamas, Barlaam and thinkers of his kind considered such secular studies essential in order to avoid ignorance of both human and divine things. But for the oriental monastic tradition stemming from Evagrius (fourth c.) and Maximus (seventh c.), "unknowing" (*agnoia* or *agnōsia*) denotes self-emptying, a voiding of the mind, so as to be filled with the grace of supernatural understanding. It is Palamas's contention that such "ignorance" is a higher state of cognition than the merely intellectual knowledge of the Greek savant.

However, it is probable that for polemical purposes, Palamas heightened the distinction between himself as champion of the contemplative tradition and Barlaam as an intellectual "positivist". Barlaam certainly seems to have neglected the mystical aspect of Christianity, but could hardly have denied it. At an earlier date (according to Nicephorus Gregoras), he had been invited to lecture on the mystical theologian Pseudo-Denys at a monastic school in Constantinople, which suggests that his orthodoxy was never called into question before the controversy with Palamas. There is no evidence that he ever denied the authority of Scripture or of the dogmatic tradition, and this of course implies acceptance of mysteries of faith not capable of positive demon-

NOTES

stration. A more balanced assessment might be that he was above all a philosophical theologian who made insufficient allowance for direct mystical vision or experiential knowledge.

In patristic usage, these two modes of cognition (mystical and intellectual) correspond to two different human cognitive faculties: the *nous*, the spiritual mind or intuitive intellect, capable of direct apprehension of the truth of things; and the *dianoia*, the analytical and discursive intellect that works out problems by logical stages and knows *about* things. In this translation, I have tried consistently to use the word "mind" for *nous* (rather than "intellect", which has a rather hard, conceptual ring in modern usage); but "mind" today is a rather imprecise word, and the reader should beware of understanding it in the sense of *dianoia*.

4. "Knowledge of beings" (*gnōsis tōn ontōn*): for Barlaam, this would appear to mean positive understanding of the character of created things, attainable through intellectual enquiry. I suspect he tended to confuse or even identify this kind of scientific knowledge of nature with the "natural contemplation" (*physikē theōria*) of the spiritual tradition (as particularly in the teaching of Maximus), whereby man's inner eye, illumined by grace, perceives the inner principle, purpose and end, *logos*, of each thing in the divine plan, i.e., comes to see the created world through God's eyes. We should note that the Barlaamites (as Palamas admits) are concerned not only with scientific study of natural phenomena, but also with understanding the inner principles (*logoi*) of things as they exist in the divine Mind. So Palamas and Barlaam seem basically at one on the desirability of "natural contemplation"; the difference is that Palamas denies secular studies are a *necessary prologue* to such deeper insight.

5. A fundamental postulate for Barlaam, in whose thought negative theology becomes a species of philosophy, an intellectual technique to establish divine transcendence by stating what God is *not*. The *via negativa* for him thus remains negative, rather than a way of initiation into mystical knowledge.

Since God is utterly unknowable in Himself, direct personal apprehension of Him is exceptional. Rather, the Creator is basically to be known (through inference, indirectly) by reflecting on His works in creation. This is of course why Barlaam considers that the secular sciences are a necessary way into theology. It would certainly not be fair to describe Barlaam as an agnostic (he accepted all the traditional doctrinal formulations); but he was little open to the dimension of continuing personal experience of God.

6. The Barlaamites are here made to offer further religious justification for their study of astronomy and other "mysteries of nature": It is by progress in knowledge that man is assimilated to God (a very intellectualist view of salvation). The mind of man (because it is created in the divine Image) contains images of the causes of things, which preexist in the mind of the Cre-

NOTES

ator. By nurturing these germs of understanding with knowledge of the natural world, man necessarily grows in wisdom, and so becomes conformed more closely to God.

7. 1 Pet. 3:15.

8. *Sensible (aisthēton)*, i.e., capable of sense perception, as opposed to *intelligible (noēton)*, apprehended by the mind (*noūs*) alone. Because this pair of words pertains to a fundamental distinction in Platonism between the world of appearances and becoming and the world of changeless and transcendent paradigms, I retain "sensible/intelligible" as technical terms in this translation.

9. In what precedes this passage, Palamas has gone on to criticise the teachings of the Greek philosophers. "These people" refers to the pagan philosophers rather than to their fourteenth-century disciples.

10. That is, the fact that rational men have so easily been led into the fundamental error of polytheism proves that the possession of reason does not of itself suffice to bring us to right ideas about God. For Palamas, polytheism is a demonic delusion, the demons themselves being taken for gods.

11. That is, not in reality, but only in the minds of the pagans. God can never actually be deprived of His eternal sovereignty, whatever man may falsely think.

12. He here attacks pagan idolatry, and in particular the idea that lifeless cult statues can become endowed with a higher or divine soul.

13. That is, angels or demons.

14. For the Christian tradition, God alone is unoriginate, and the source of all being. The basic sin of idolatry is to rob God of the worship that belongs to Him alone, and to apply it to creatures.

15. See note 12, above.

16. 1 Cor. 2:4.

17. 1 Cor. 2:13.

18. 1 Cor. 1:26.

19. Rom. 1:22.

20. 1 Cor. 1:20.

21. *Loc. cit.*

22. Cf. 1 Cor. 1:28.

23. Col. 2:8.

24. 1 Cor. 2:6.

25. That is, a patristic writer. We have been unable to trace the source of this quotation.

26. That is, just as the body fails without appropriate natural food, so the soul atrophies without that supernatural life (a gift of grace, unobtainable through human intellection) which is its proper nourishment.

27. A very important admission on the part of Palamas, who here explicitly accepts the legitimacy of philosophy and the natural sciences *within their*

NOTES

proper limits. He is not an obscurantist, and has no wish to prevent Christians from using their God-given intellects to explore and understand the created order. His quarrel is with those who make inflated claims for the scope of the human mind and who arrogantly deny the authenticity of contemplative experience. The gift of reason is an endowment itself good, but eminently capable of perversion (as in the case of demons, some pagan philosophers, and heretics). Palamas also insists that while such secular studies may be appropriate for laymen, they are unnecessary for monks. In the case of religious knowledge (the goal of the ascetic life), direct experience has a primacy over speculation and science.

28. Jas. 3:15.

29. Even pagan philosophy is not entirely devoid of truth, but this must be carefully sifted out (a perilous undertaking, since heresy results from the absorption of alien elements in Greek philosophy into the Christian tradition).

30. Palamas uses the image of the serpent's flesh as medicine in I.i.11 and II.i.15–16, and also in his Second Letter to Barlaam (Coisl. 100, f. 98).

31. In Palamas's view, Barlaam and his followers considered scientific knowledge of the natural world (rather than contemplative insight) the way to spiritual knowledge, and claimed that it is only through such "natural" knowledge that we are assimilated to God.

32. Gen. 4:7 (LXX). The quotation continues, "have you not sinned?"

33. The spiritual senses: an important theme in patristic spirituality, deriving ultimately from the mystical exegesis of the Song of Songs, beginning with Origen (e.g., *Com. in Cant.* I.2 and 4; *hom. in Cant.* II.4). In the course of spiritual maturation, the soul must develop faculties analogous to the sense organs of the body, with which to perceive and discern the things of God— e.g., an inner eye that "sees" the hand of God in creation, or in the events of history.

34. The Greek translation of the writings of St. Isaac, Nestorian bishop of Nineveh (seventh c.) was venerated as one of the major sources of hesychast spirituality. The quotation here is from *hom.* 72 (ed. Theotokis (Leipsig, 1770), p. 463; ed. Spetsieri (Athens, 1895), p. 314).

35. For Gregory, contemplation of God's works in creation through prayer is a much safer "natural philosophy" than the study of the Greek philosophers. But, for him, study of nature should pass into praise of the Creator; and through prayer, natural knowledge is deepened into an insight into the mysteries of God, unobtainable by reason alone.

36. 1 Cor. 2:9.

37. That is, it is not a supernatural gift, for reason unaided by grace can attain to such knowledge. Cf. Section 19 above, where Palamas does call philosophy "insofar as it is natural" a gift of God.

38. 2 Cor. 1:12.

NOTES

39. 1 Cor. 1:26.

40. Cf. 1 Tim. 3:7. The "outside (exōthen) philosophy" is a frequent phrase in the Fathers to refer to the pagan philosophers of the Greco-Roman world.

41. Cf. *Hom.* XLI.14 (PG 36, 448C).

42. Cf. Acts 13:19.

43. 2 Cor. 12:2–4.

44. 1 Cor. 2:6.

45. Jn. 1:29.

46. 1 Cor. 1:18.

B. Apophatic theology as positive experience

1. Col. 2:18 (variant).

2. That is, the theophanies of the Old Testament were symbolic, those of the New actual—not in itself a contradictory view.

3. For Barlaam's account of the spiritual practices of the hesychasts, *vid. Ep.* V, to Ignatius (ed. Schirò, pp. 323–324).

4. An unworthy suggestion of skullduggery! In fact, Barlaam says that in becoming for a while the pupil of the monks, he wished only to accept the best of their teaching (Schirò, *ibid.*, p. 322). We may well suppose that certain neo-Messalian excesses were current in *some* quarters, towards which B. was right to adopt a critical attitude.

5. Cf. *ibid.*, p. 323.

6. Barlaam, *Ep.* III, to Palamas (*ibid.*, p. 281).

7. Cf. Ps. Denys, *de div. nom.* I. 5, PG III, 593B, and Evagrius, *de orat.* 113, PG LXXIX, 1192D.

8. That is, the divine uncreated light of Thabor, God Himself in His outward manifestation (or *energies*).

9. A key idea in Palamas, deriving ultimately from Ps. Denys (e.g., *de myst. theol.* I. 1, PG III, 997A): The Divine Reality transcends not only the positive concepts we may hold of God (cataphatic theology), but also the negations of the apophatic way. The "knowledge" of the utterly unknowable God is a supremely positive experience, not a cognitive void; for it is the superabundance of light and being in God that dazzles the created mind. God, as Denys says, is beyond unknowability (*hyperagnōstos*), beyond the human antithesis of affirmation and negation. Similarly the vision of such a God must be ineffable; yet it is less misleading to say what it is not than what it is.

10. Judg. 13:17–18.

11. The vision of God for Palamas is not an intellectual grasp of an external object, but an interior participation in the life of the Holy Spirit: to see God is to share in this life, i.e., become divinised. This involves a complete transfiguration of the whole person, body and soul together.

12. Jn. 17:22, 24.

NOTES

13. That is, the transfigured spiritual intellect is able to apprehend directly the transcendent realities figured forth symbolically in Scripture and the Liturgy.

14. That is, Ps. Denys, the author of the treatise *Concerning the Celestial Hierarchy.*

15. Ps. Denys, *de coel. hier.,* VII.2, PG III, 208BC, and *de div. nom.,* I.4, *ibid.,* 592BC.

16. Cf. *hom.* XII.14, PG XXXIV, 565BC.

17. St. Andrew of Crete, *hom. VII in Transfig.,* PG XCVII, 933C.

18. 2 Cor. 12:2. Paul's ecstasy is frequently cited by the Greek Fathers as a paradigm of mystical experience (e.g., Maximus, *Ambig.,* PG XCI, 1076BC, 1114C, and *Cent.* V.85, PG XC, 1384D.)

19. Cf. *In Cant. hom.* IV, PG XLIV, 833CD, and VII, *ibid.* 920BC. Gregory of Nyssa points out that the inexhaustibility of the vision of God is a function not only of human limitations but of the transcendent fullness and infinity of the Divine Nature.

20. Palamas here points to a central paradox of Christian experience: that the Holy Spirit, Who is the very milieu of the believer's innermost life, is also the most elusive and intangible of realities. He as it were effaces Himself to make known the Father through the Son.

21. *De div. nom.,* I.5, PG III, 593C.

22. That is, there must be a stripping of the mind (which does require human effort), a kind of mental *ascesis,* in order that God, Who transcends all concepts (and their negations), may freely make Himself known. One must not confound the apophatic preparation with the ineffable divine gift.

23. Ep. IV (ed. Theotoki, p. 576). The Messalian heretics seem to have believed that progress in the vision of God was simply a matter of the spiritual prowess of the believer, in which grace played little part. Fr. Hausherr (in *Orientalia Christiana Periodica* I, 1935, pp. 328–360) has rightly drawn a parallel with the error of the Pelagians, though in this case it is more a question of an activism of prayer than of outward works.

24. *Ecstasis* in the Greek Fathers need not imply any kind of paranormal psychological state or loss of consciousness. It is (literally) a "going-out" from oneself, a self-transcendence under the influence of love and divine grace. It enables a supernatural mode of cognition of divine things, which is mystical knowledge, after one has ceased to know and see through the functions of the discursive intellect and the senses.

25. A technical phrase deriving from Evagrius, "pure prayer" means the state of undifferentiated consciousness when the mind is "naked" of all images and earthly notions. But, Palamas insists, it is not enough to abstract oneself from creation; the mind must be emptied of contingent things so as to be filled with divine ones. He draws a parallel with the moral life: The extirpation of the passions and achievement of "purity of heart" are not matters of

NOTES

static impassivity but opening up of the self to the inexhaustible life of Heaven.

26. Cf. *Ep.* V, PG III, 1073A.

27. Cf. Matt. 7:6 ("pearls before swine").

28. Cf. *de myst. theol.* III, PG III, 1033B.

29. Cf. *ibid.* 1033C.

30. The cardinal point about the *via negativa* is that it is neither a species of agnosticism nor itself the vision of God, but rather a necessary preliminary process of mental detachment from created things which provides an image of the otherness of divine ones.

31. This moral note reappears time and again in the *Triads:* First and foremost the knowledge of God is not an intellectual matter (in the modern sense), but is acquired by grace and obedience to God's commands.

32. In fact, the phrase "divine sense" (*aisthēsis theia*) is an Origenist version of Prov. 2:5 (LXX: *epignōsis theou*). On the "spiritual senses", see note 33, Section A. The primary exegesis of this key idea of Eastern Christian spirituality is in Gregory of Nyssa (*In Cant. hom.* I, PG XLIV, 780C).

33. *De div. nom.* VII.1, PG III, 865C.

34. *Ibid.* IV.11, PG III, 708D.

35. Cf. *Cap. theol.* 2, 70, 76; PG XC, 1156, 1160.

36. Or "perception". Yet it is neither intellection nor sense perception, but transcendental knowledge, directly infused by the Holy Spirit alone.

37. Cf. 2 Cor. 12:2.

38. *Vid.* note 24, above, on ecstasy.

39. *Hom.* 32, ed. Theotoki, p. 206. Isaac is presumably citing Gregory of Nazianzus, though the language is also very reminiscent of Evagrius.

40. *Ibid.*

41. The image of becoming "all eye", entirely subsumed in the vision that consumes and unites, goes back to Plotinus.

42. Cf. Macarius-Symeon, *de libert. mentis* 21, PG XXXIV, 956A.

43. An episode in the *Life* of St. Benedict (PL. LXVI, 197B), whose biography was popular among Byzantine monks. At a time of theological tension between Latins and Greeks, it is pleasing to find Palamas describing a Western saint as "one of the most perfect". Cf. E. Lanne, "L'interprétation palamite de la vision de Saint Benoit", *Le Millénaire du mont Athos, 963–1963,* II (Venice/Chévetogne, 1965), pp. 21–47.

44. That is, the vision of God does not belong to creatures, as their natural property.

45. Palamas here takes up another leading theme of Gregory of Nyssa: *epektasis,* the inexhaustible character of the vision of God as rooted in the infinite nature of the Divine. Even in the Age to Come, there can be no end to the good things that God has to reveal; so the soul is always *in via,* always moving on.

NOTES

46. This touches on the cardinal doctrine of Palamas, that God, utterly and permanently unknowable and inaccessible in His essence, yet comes to us and shares His life with us in His energies. Palamas insists that the energies *are* God, personally present, not just a created grace in us; yet also affirms that the energies are distinct from the essence, without implying division in God.

47. The language in this paragraph is Dionysian (cf. *de div. nom.*, XI.6, II.11, V.8, PG III, 956A, 649A, 824A). The light, energy or grace is indeed "divinity", a communication of the life of God; yet God as the source of that life may be termed "beyond being", or even "beyond divinity" (*hypertheos*).

48. *Epist.* 2, PG III, 1068–1069A.

C. The Hesychast method of prayer, and the transformation of the body

1. 1 Cor. 6:19.

2. Cf. Heb. 3:6.

3. 2 Cor. 6:16.

4. This is the Manichaean (or Bogomil) view, also to be found in Byzantine Messalianism. It will be remembered that Barlaam had accused the hesychasts of Messalianism (*Ep.* V, ed. Schirò, p. 324). According to the mediaeval Manichees, the material cosmos (including the human body) was the evil fabrication of the Devil.

5. A fundamental assertion of Christian orthodoxy. Even the most platonic of the Church Fathers admit this (e.g., Ps. Denys, *de div. nom.* IV. 27, PG III, 728CD). The body, assumed by Christ in becoming man, is inherently good, but liable to corruption as a result of the perversion of the will away from God.

6. Rom. 7:24.

7. *Ibid.* 14.

8. *Ibid.* 18.

9. *Ibid.* 23.

10. *Ibid.* 2.

11. *nēpsis*, vigilance, spiritual attentiveness or sobriety; maintaining watch over the heart and mind (*nous*). This is a central concept of hesychasm (the Greek title of the *Philocalia*, the basic *corpus* of texts on interior prayer, is "the Philocalia of the *neptic* Fathers").

12. It is important to note that Orthodox asceticism does not command the extirpation of natural desires, but rather their harmonious reordering towards a higher end (cf. II.ii.19, *infra*).

13. 2 Cor. 4:6.

14. *Ibid.* 7.

15. Or "person" (Greek *prosōpon*).

NOTES

16. A specific mode of "guarding the mind" by inner attention is to re-call it *within* the body, so that the praying mind does not get distracted by errant thoughts (see I.ii.3, below).

17. *Noūs*, spiritual mind or intellect; often contrasted with the discour-sive reason (*dianoia*)—though Palamas does not make this distinction consis-tently).

18. Cf. Gregory of Nyssa, *de opif.* XII, PG XLIV, 156CD.

19. Palamas is thinking primarily here of Ps. Macarius, mentioned in the next paragraph.

20. "Breath of [animal] soul" (*psychikon pneuma*) refers to the nonratio-nal life force, the instinctual drives, that we share with the animals. This low-er soul is to be harmonised and brought under control of the higher part of the soul in the heart. (See the words of Macarius, quoted a few lines below, p. 43.)

21. Mt. 15:11.

22. *Ibid.* 19.

23. Hom. XV.20 (PG XXIV, 589B); ed. H. Dörries (Berlin, 1964), p. 139.

24. *Heart (kardia)* in the Greek tradition is not just the physical organ, or the affections and emotions, but the spiritual centre of man's being, his in-most self, where the encounter with God takes place.

25. *Or,* "recollect", i.e., concentrate and reintegrate the distracted mind, which is so easily deflected from inner attention on God. The whole purpose of the Jesus Prayer is to achieve this interior recollection, by "bringing the mind into the heart".

26. Because his name means "blessed" in Greek.

27. Cf. *hom.* XV.20.

28. Ps. 44:14 (LXX text). The application of this verse to the interior life goes back to Origen, *Selecta in Pss.*, PG XII, 1432C; cf. Basil, *hom. in Ps. XLIV,* PG XXIX, 412AB, and Diadochus, *Cap.* 79 (ed. Des Places, p. 137).

29. Gal. 4:6.

30. Lk. 17:21.

31. Prov. 27:21 (version of Origen).

32. Prov. 2:5. "Spiritual" in Greek here is *noera*. "Intellectual" might be an alternative translation, but I prefer spiritual because of the connection with the notion of the "spiritual senses". *Noeros* tends to be the active epithet from *noūs* (the spiritual intellect), i.e., that which belongs to *noūs*, the appre-hend*ing* power (as against *noētos*, that which is apprehend*ed* or intelligible).

33. *Or,* "is clothed (or enwrapped) in" (the verb can be either middle or passive).

34. St. John Climacus, *Scala* XXVI.26 (PG LXXXVIII, 1020A). There can be no end to the search for spiritual understanding (*aisthēsis noera*), the cultivation of the sense of God and of the divine dimension in ourselves and in creation.

NOTES

35. Cf. 2 Cor. 1:22, 5:5; Eph. 1:4.

36. In a truly incarnational spirituality, the body is never regarded as alien to the soul in its spiritual progress, for the whole man, body as well as soul, must be transformed and divinised. This is the fundamental Christian correction of the dualism of much Greek thought, especially Platonism.

37. Palamas here invokes the pejorative sense of *ecstasis,* loss of self-control, madness, demonic possession.

38. 1 Tim. 6:20.

39. *Hom. XII in Prov.,* 7, PG XXXI, 401A.

40. The author is not, of course, making a generalisation about the mind, but referring only to those who dare to put themselves forward as spiritual teachers, yet lack self-knowledge and awareness of their own inner impoverishment.

41. *de div. nom.* IV.9, PG III, 705B.

42. *Ibid.,* 705A. Ps. Denys is here speaking of the angels ("divine intelligences") who, when concentrated on God, move in the *circle* of eternity, but when going outside the heavenly sphere, move down "in a straight line" to assist those in our lower world.

43. Ep. II.2, PG XXXII, 228A.

44. *De div. nom., loc. cit.* The point here is that recollection and awareness are essential prerequisites of the spiritual way; it is through distraction that the Devil turns us aside from the path.

45. Cf. Barlaam, Ep. IV to Ignatius (ed. Schirò, p. 315).

46. Cf. *Scala* XXVII, PG LXXXVIII, 1097B.

47. Before the Incarnation, Christ as divine Logos penetrated and was immanent in the cosmos as Creator. But by taking on a body, He has established a new relation with creation, and given all matter a new potential as vehicle of the Spirit. The underlying notion of "natural form" is presumably Aristotelian, referring to the soul as "form" (*eidos*) of the body. Christ, by assuming a human soul, has the same relation to matter *qua* man that any ensouled person has; so that man, by recollecting the soul in the body, can mirror Christ's relation to the universe in a way impossible before the Incarnation.

48. Palamas here recalls the Platonic antithesis between the simple unitary nature of the soul and the multiple and composite character of the body. In the corrected Platonism of the Greek Fathers, the body, though not initially corruptible, has become liable to fragmentation and decay as a result of the Fall (the word here translated "divisibility" contains also the notion of discontinuity). While matter remains inert, it constitutes a barrier and burden to the soul, but once revitalised by the Spirit, and conformed to the model of the Incarnate Christ, it becomes a supple instrument of the spirit. The element of discontinuity is overcome in the work of sanctification; this is why the union

NOTES

of heavenly and earthly in Christ must be the paradigm for all Christian spiritual life.

49. That is, Climacus.

50. Palamas is here referring to the psychophysical method taught by earlier hesychastic masters such as Ps. Symeon and Nicephorus. He is careful not to overemphasise the breathing exercises: These are not essential to progress in interior prayer, but may be helpful for beginners, under proper supervision. For a translation of the *Method* ascribed to Symeon, *vid.* J. Gouillard, *Petite Philocalie* (Paris, 1953), pp. 207–220. "To look [at themselves]—*blepein*, not *theōrein* (to contemplate)—in this context probably has the literal sense of fixing the gaze on the navel.

51. Because the mind is ever active, it must be given *some* work to do, even at the time of prayer. Thus, most typically, the hesychastic masters recommend invocation of the Name of Jesus as a focus of concentration upon God, the repetition of the Name being regulated by the inhalation and exhalation of the breath. *Vid.* Kallistos Ware, ed., *The Art of Prayer* (London, 1966), introd., esp. pp. 27–37.

52. As recommended by Ps. Symeon, *Method* (ed. Hausherr, *Orientalia Christiana Analecta*, IX.2, p. 164), but not by Nicephorus (cf. II.ii.25, below).

53. Cf. Ps. Denys, *de div. nom.* IV.9, PG III, 705A.

54. This is the basic meaning of the Greek word *hesychia*, from which our term hesychasm derives. A hesychast is thus one who practises inner stillness or quiet.

55. It would seem to be a common experience of Eastern Christian contemplatives that initially one has to exercise persistence and real effort, and force the lips to repeat the Jesus Prayer; but in time, the prayer becomes gradually internalised, and finally self-activating as an unceasing rhythm within the heart, even during sleep.

56. 1 Cor. 13:7.

57. Cf. Ps. Macarius, Hom. XVI.7, PG XXXIV, 617D (ed. H. Dörries [Berlin, 1964], p. 163); St. John Climacus, *Scala* XXV and XXVII, PG LXXXVIII, 1000Df. and 1133B.

58. Cf. Ps. Denys, *de div. nom.* IV.8, PG III, 704D. *Vid.* note 42, above.

59. Cf. Ps. Symeon, *Method,* ed. I. Hausherr, p. 164. (Palamas again describes this psychophysical method, which is in some ways comparable to that employed in *yoga,* in his Letter II to Barlaam.) The fixing of the gaze on the centre point of the body directs the attention in upon the self (or "heart"), and away from the distraction of external impressions. The practice of the hesychasts of contemplating with the eyes fixed on the navel gave rise to the sobriquet *omphalopsychoi* ("people-having-their-soul-in-their-navel") among their detractors, a "calumny" dealt with by Palamas in I.ii.10.

60. According to mediaeval notions, the power of concupiscence is con-

centrated in the belly (hence the reference to the "law of sin" that rules there and the use of the strong word *thēr* (wild beast) for "intelligible *animal*"). By fixing attention on this "lower half", the contemplative as it were descends to do battle in the area where evil is centred. Alternatively, "beast" may refer to the Devil, whose seductive powers are concentrated in the belly.

61. Cf. Rom. 6:23.

62. Tit. 3:5.

63. Lk. 11:26.

64. Deut. 15:9.

65. *loc. cit.*

66. Eccles. 10:4.

67. Ps. 7:10; Rev. 1:23.

68. 1 Cor. 11:41.

69. Ps. 138:12–13.

70. That is, the integration of the whole man through interior prayer has the effect of cleansing and transforming all the natural faculties. See note 12, above.

71. Gen. 6:2.

72. Although it is necessary to exclude external sensations at the time of prayer, there is no need to strive for an eradication of *all* the dispositions or moods evoked in us by our life in the world. Charitable feelings, for instance, are actually conducive to prayer. At the same time, the Orthodox tradition always teaches that one should simplify the mind as far as possible in meditation. The aim of "pure prayer" is not to have good thoughts *about* God but to achieve direct awareness of His presence.

73. That is, the beneficial suffering occasioned by fasting, vigils and similar ascetic practices.

74. Cf. 1 Cor. 8:1.

75. Asceticism is never an end in itself, but a discipline that frees a man from the tyranny of the passions, so enabling him to devote himself without distraction to his "inner work" (*ergasia noera*).

76. Compunction (*katanyxis*): a state of deep penitence springing from awareness of sinfulness and of God's mercy.

77. Ps. 51 (50):19.

78. Hom. XXIV.11, PG XXXV, 1181B.

79. Mt. 17:21, Mk. 9:29.

80. *Analgēsia*—lit., incapability of feeling pain, i.e., spiritual blindness or obtuseness: not to be confused with impassibility, control of the disordered passions, or purity of heart. Impassibility does not consist in not experiencing the cost of discipline; indeed, without *catharsis* (purging of body and soul), one cannot attain to this inner freedom.

81. For example, St. Maximus, *Ambig.*, PG XCI, 1344C. (Cf. Mk. 3:5,

NOTES

5:52; Jn. 12:40, "hardness of heart"); also St. John Climacus, *Scala* 6, PG LXXXVIII, 796 B.

82. St. John Climacus, *ibid.*, 14, 865D.

83. St. John Climacus, *ibid.*, 6, 796B.

84. *Ibid.*, 28, 1129A.

85. It is only in the highest reaches of interior contemplation that one is unaware of the suffering of *askesis*. Barlaam fails to realise (through lack of experience) that without suffering one does not attain to the vision of God.

86. Mark the Monk, *de lege spir.* 12, PG LXV, 908A.

87. 2 Cor. 12:2.

88. *De myst. theol.* I.3, PG III, 1000C.

89. Presumably referring to the vision of the uncreated light of the Trinity, which Barlaam blasphemously dismisses as a product of the imagination. According to him, all that is seen is a false image of the heart itself.

90. Gen. 6:3.

91. Just as carnal pleasures infect the soul, so the vision of God transforms the body; indeed, the resurrection of the body is anticipated on earth by those who attain true knowledge of God—but this *gnosis* can only be a matter of *experience*, not of intellection.

92. Jn. 3:6,8.

93. *Lit.*, "to *suffer* divine things". Cf. Ps. Denys's definition of religious knowledge, "Not to learn but to suffer" (i.e., experience).

94. The sensitive faculty of the soul is unitary, but capable of experiencing impressions either from above (religious experience, which it mediates to the body), or from below (corporeal and sensual experiences deriving from the body). In the latter case, the soul is dragged down and debased; in the former, its "passionate part" (*pathētikon*) finds its *true* (spiritual) fulfillment.

95. Acts 6:15.

96. Ps. 46 (47):10.

97. Palamas is obviously thinking here of his opponent, Barlaam, a "philosopher" who lacks the hesychasts' direct experiential knowledge of the transforming effect of uncreated grace in the body. As a result, he tends to lapse into a dualistic anthropology, which excludes the body from the process of divinisation.

98. Matt. 7:7.

99. 2 Cor. 12:2.

100. 1 Cor. 12:10.

101. Cf. *ibid.* 14:26, 12:8.

102. *Ibid.* 12:9.

103. *Ibid.* 12:10.

104. 2 Tim. 1:6.

105. Cf. Acts 8:17 (the Spirit conveyed by laying-on of hands). Palamas's

point here is that the body may be a vehicle of grace, even when the soul is not in an elevated spiritual state. It is, of course, a basic principle of sacramental teaching that the efficacy of the sacraments does not depend on the worthiness of the celebrant.

106. Palamas is primarily thinking again of the mystical experience of Paul (2 Cor. 12:2). Two points are being made about *ecstasis:* first, that it is a matter of transcending (lit., "going out from") one's *whole* nature, not just from the body, and secondly, it is in and through the whole created nature that God effects such ineffable things.

107. In fact, in an upper room (Acts 1:13). Palamas is probably confusing the Pentecost narrative with Acts 2:46 or Luke 24:53.

108. Acts 1:14.

109. Acts 2:1–4.

110. Ex 14:14–15. (Moses is ordered by God to part the waters of the Red Sea with his staff). Cf. Gregory Nazianzen, *hom.* XVI. 4, PG XXV, 937A, and Basil, *In Ps. CXIV*, PG XXIX, 485C.

111. This is really special pleading on the part of Palamas, since Barlaam is speaking specifically of ecstasy, not of prayer in general. Barlaam would hardly have denied the ancient monastic tradition that manual work should be accompanied by prayer, or that "memory of God" should pervade all outward activity of the recollected man.

112. The idea of the subjection of the passionate parts of the soul to the governance of reason (*to hēgemonikon* or *logistikon*) derives from Plato's myth of the Charioteer (*Phaedrus* 246Af.; cf. *Rep.* IV, 434Dff.), as does the division of the lower faculties of the soul into *thymikon* (irascible or incensive) and *to epithumētikon*, (concupiscent or desiring, appetitive).

113. 1 Cor. 1:20. Palamas is not decrying the natural sciences (lit., "knowledge of beings"), but their misuse, e.g., using speculative reason to construct hypotheses contrary to the data of revelation.

114. That is, the passions, redirected towards divine things, provide the affective drive or élan that energises the ascent to God. Thus, for example, the irascible urge can be transformed into righteous wrath and a passion for justice; and above all (a point made in passing by Palamas, but much dwelt upon by Origen and Gregory of Nyssa), *eros*, the passionate aspect of love, can be turned away from carnality towards an intense desire for communion with Christ, the bridegroom of the soul.

115. "Remembrance of God": a state of continuous recollectedness in which attention is centered on God. As a basic aspect of "pure" prayer, this notion is a constant in Eastern Christian spiritual teaching. It first becomes explicitly linked with the invocation of the Name of Jesus in Diadochus of Photice, fifth century (e.g., *Centuries*, ch. XCVII, ed. Des Places, p. 159). Cf. St. John Climacus, *Scala* XXVII, PG LXXXVIII, 1112C.

116. Cf. Jn. 4:19, 5:1–2, etc.

NOTES

117. The way to perfect love is through dispassion, seen positively as stability in the good. Once the passions are exercised in accordance with their original purity, and a man is freed from the struggles against his own disordered nature, he is free to exercise active love towards God and his fellows. In this sense, "impassibility" is highly compatible with charity, and will doubtless involve suffering on other people's behalf.

118. *Sc.*, violence against the self, the force initially necessary to discipline the fallen nature. (This is the point of the *askesis* of the monk, mentioned in the first paragraph.) But all must struggle to acquire habitual good dispositions, whether in the world or in the cloister.

119. Rom. 12:1.

120. Prov. 12:13.

121. Ps. 102 (103):18.

122. Jas. 1:25.

D. Deification in Christ

1. On the divine essence as transcending negation as well as affirmation, see above, Section B, notes 9 and 49. Insofar as "God" is a summation of positive notions we hold about the deity, God must be "beyond-God", a supereminent "dazzling darkness".

2. "Hypostatic" in the sense of a concrete, objective reality, not something imagined by the subjective mind. The use of the word here is not to be confused with hypostasis *qua* one of the Persons in the Trinity. The uncreated light or energy of God does not constitute a fourth hypostasis in God (*quartum quid*), as Latin critics have sometimes suggested.

3. The divine light is really seen, but only by the spiritually transfigured eyes of the saints.

4. A classic example of deliberately paradoxical language, of the kind common in Gregory of Nyssa and Ps. Denys (cf. "learned ignorance", "sober drunkenness") when referring to mystical knowledge or experience.

5. The divine subject of such illumination constitutes an overwhelming experiential impact, yet permanently defies intellectual analysis. True mystical cognition is darkness to the discursive mind (*dianoia*), since it is by definition ineffable and incomprehensible.

6. Cf. the famous definition of St. Basil: "The essence remains unapproachable (*aprositos*), but the energies come down to us" (*Ep.* 234, 1). The divine light *is* God insofar as He is knowable, yet God remains transcendent even in His self-manifestation, evoking *ecstasis*, self-transcendence, in those to whom He appears.

7. The visible transfiguration of the saint's body (a prefiguration of the glorification of the resurrected body at the Last Day) is quite frequently attested in early monastic sources (e.g. *Apoph. Patrum*, Joseph of Panephysis, 7;

NOTES

Silvanus, 12 ("his face and body shining like an angel"); Arsenius, 27 (the old man appeared "entirely like a flame").

8. On the hesychastic master Arsenius, *vid.* the eulogy by St. Theodore Studites, *Orat.* XII, PG XCIX, 860B, and J. Hausherr, *L'hésychasme* ... in *Orientalia Christiana Periodica* XII (1956) 25–7.

9. Acts 6:15 ("his face was like the face of an angel"). In fact, this was during his trial, not during his execution.

10. Ex. 34:29 ("the skin of his face shone because he had been talking with God").

11. 2 Cor. 12:4 ("he heard things ineffable").

12. *Hom.* XLV, 11, PG XXXVI, 637B.

13. Ex. 16:14ff.

14. Addressing Barlaam directly, who was prepared to acept the hesychasts' claim to have seen the divine light if this were admitted to be an angel.

15. Num. 22:25, 27.

16. The vision of God in the mirror of the purified soul is a commonplace of patristic spiritual teaching. The doctrine stems from the biblical view of man as created in the divine image and therefore originally capable of reflecting the splendour of God Himself. But, as a result of the Fall, the image has become tarnished and corroded, and must undergo restoration and cleaning (*katharsis*) in order once again to mediate the vision of God. Barlaam (above, Section 7) shows himself perfectly familiar with traditional (especially Evagrian) teaching on this point.

17. There would seem to be little at issue between Palamas and Barlaam here. Barlaam states, "The mind (*noūs*) when purified of passion and ignorance, *sees God* in His own image" (II.iii.7). But Palamas is at pains to emphasise the crucial point that this vision is the fruit of grace, not some merely natural and self-generated illumination of the mind, as claimed by Barlaam.

18. Palamas is here understanding "ignorance" in a positivist sense, i.e., lack of education in the profane sciences (*vid.* Section A, I.i,q., above, Barlaam's alleged views on the necessity of monks' acquiring Greek culture, in order to attain knowledge of God through "knowing beings"). Palamas insists that such knowledge is quite superfluous for progress in the spiritual life, and may actually impede it.

19. It is, of course, dubious whether the hesychasts *did* ever equate the uncreated light with the divine essence, as the Messalians apparently did.

20. For example, Ps. Denys, *de eccl. hier.* II, PG III, 392A.

21. Isaac of Nineveh, *hom.* 72 (ed. N. Theotokis, p. 415).

22. That is, he contrasts two kinds of religious knowledge: "natural contemplation" (*physike theōria*), knowledge of God in creation; and direct vision of God's uncreated energies or "glory" (*theologia* in the strict sense).

23. Jn. 12:24.

NOTES

24. *Ibid.*, 15.

25. *Vid.* note 6 above, and cf. Ps. Denys, *de myst. theol.* V, PG III, 1048A. The "glory" would not be divine if it were merely one among a number of intelligible objects in the world. As uncreated, it "is not", i.e., it is necessarily transcendent, and yet mysteriously distinct from (though inseparable from) the Divine "Nature" (i.e., essence).

26. That is, the created (and therefore composite) human nature united to Christ as Second Person (*hypostasis*) of the Trinity. Participation in Christ's divine glory is not limited to His own individual humanity, but is shared by those incorporated into His Body by grace.

27. Jn. 17:22–23.

28. *Ibid.*, 24.

29. That is, the learned man, who knows about the laws of nature, has not necessarily advanced to infused knowledge of God. At best, through natural theology, God is only known analogically and indirectly. However, we should remember that in the Greek tradition "natural contemplation" often goes beyond deducing the power and wisdom of God from His "vestiges" in creation; it involves contemplating things through the eyes of God, intuitively seeing their inner principles through the power of the spiritual intellect (*noūs*).

30. A fundamental principle for orthodoxy: sanctification, true knowledge of God, is not acquired by intellectual prowess or erudition but by humble obedience (cf. Section 17, *infra*).

31. Jn. 14:23.

32. *Ibid.*, 21.

33. *loc. cit.*

34. In the sense of a field of human knowledge (*epistēmē*) naturally accessible to the reason. Infused illumination (the true *gnosis*) is different in kind from that sort of knowledge, and as such is "not-knowledge", or "learned ignorance". It is in this respect that Palamas affirms that "contemplation is not knowledge".

35. *Vid.* II.i.34, 37, and note 18, above.

36. That is, mystical knowledge is inaccessible to the unillumined created mind; it is transcendent, unique, not to be compared with any other kind of knowledge.

37. Isaac of Nineveh, cited Section 15 (cf. note 21).

38. Other patristic writers apply the title "paternity" to Christ to illustrate His saving role as Second Adam, citing in particular Isa. 8:16 (cf. Jn. 2:29). *Vid.*, e.g., *Ep. ad Diognetum* (ed. H. I. Marrou, p. 192); also several passages in Ps. Macarius. Ps. Denys applies the notion of paternity to the Trinity as a whole, not only to the Father (*de div. nom.* I.4, PG III, 592 A).

39. Cf. Eph. 3:15. Palamas means that the representatives of the Church

133

NOTES

hierarchy are "Fathers" because they are images of Christ's paternity.

40. 2 Pet. 1:16. On St. Peter, as model of all bishops, see J. Meyendorff et al., *The Primacy of Peter in the Orthodox Church* (London; Faith Press, 1963).

41. Lk. 9:32.

42. Mt. 17:2.

43. Ps. 103 (104):2.

44. 2 Pet. 1:18.

45. *Ibid.*, 19.

46. *Ibid.*

47. *loc. cit.*

48. *loc. cit.*

49. That is, the truth of Scripture is not self-explanatory, but remains an "obscure light" until the Holy Spirit illuminates our hearts to perceive its inner meaning. By contemplation, the inner eye is purified, and we are assimilated to Christ, Who is all truth; thus the hesychast is able to see the divine light directly ("in full daylight"), not only as mediated through the veils of Scripture.

50. *De div. nom.* I.4, PG III, 592BC. The crucial identification here is of the light that illumines the Christian contemplatives on earth and saints in heaven with the Light of Thabor. It will also be the glory of the Age to Come, as Denys says: So the hesychasts who have already attained to the vision of the divine light are living eschatological lives, anticipating here and now the splendour of the Resurrection at the End. The light that transfigured Christ was an effulgence of divinity, not a product of the apostles' imagination.

51. Cf. 1 Thess. 4:17.

52. The analogy of the Sun, representing the Absolute and the light that flows from It, is a commonplace of the Greek patristic tradition, going back eventually to Plato's image in *Rep.* Palamas is at pains to point out that the metaphor cannot be pressed too far, because the sun is liable to change and its light too is variable. The reference to the sun's obeying the orders of the saints alludes to certain O.T. incidents (Jos. 10:12–13; 2 Kings 20:11) cited by Palamas in a different context in his *Letter II to Barlaam*, 61, ed. P. Chrestou, in *Palama Syggrammata* (Thessaloniki, 1962), p. 294.

53. That is, the body of the transfigured Christ in the first place, and by grace, the bodies of the saints, even in this life. The glory that can transfigure the saint here and now is no other than the radiance of the Age to Come.

54. God is a *unique* reality, and knowledge of Him necessarily transcends every mode of created knowledge. Mystical knowledge is always a gift, for it is not connatural to the *nous*, the spiritual intellect. This is why it may be termed "darkness" or "ignorance" with respect to the created mind; but (as we have seen) it exceeds negative as well as positive description, and this is properly to be received in loving silence.

55. Negative theology can remain at a purely intellectual level, as a defi-

nitional procedure. We may see the theological necessity of rejecting all the positive attributes of God as inadequate, without in any way directly *experiencing* the Hidden God. This union with God, on the other hand, requires radical conversion, involving a moral and spiritual assimilation to God (for which the stripping of the mind of concepts *about* God is a preparation); and a "going out" from the limitations of created nature under the impetus of love.

56. For example, *de div. nom.* I.5, PG III, 593BC.

57. Cf. *Triads* I.iii.7, II.iii.6.

58. St. John Climacus, *Scala* XXVIII, PG LXXXVIII, 1132D.

59. *De div. nom.* III.1, PG III, 680D, etc.

60. Pure prayer is a matter of simple attention to God, not of thinking *about* Him. Hence, we must not only rid ourselves at the time of prayer of evil thoughts prompted by the Devil, but also detach ourselves from all extraneous ideas derived from creation (cf. Evagrius, *de orat.* 56–76, pp. 66–69).

61. Cf. St. John Climacus, *Scala* XVIII, ib. 1140AB.

62. Such detachment presupposes *apatheia* in the sense that inner quiet is impossible without a certain stability in virtue and emancipation from the onslaughts of the disordered passions. Palamas calls this state *ec-stasis*, a "standing apart" from created things in order to be at the disposal of God. But it is not the ecstasy of mystical union, an entirely grace-given "ravishment" for which the soul may prepare itself but can in no way bring about by its own efforts.

63. This is the notion of *epektasis*, infinite progress in divine knowledge, so dear to Gregory of Nyssa (*vid.* his *Life of Moses*). Because God's nature is infinite and inexhaustible, there can be literally *no end* to the good things the elect soul may receive at the hands of God. To attain any peak in our ascent to Him is to open up before the inner eye yet further vistas of knowledge and love. Even in the Age to Come, then, the vision of God is not a static beholding of God *ab externo*, but a dynamic participation in the infinite fulness of God's being.

64. That is, the question of the Uncreated Light, virtually as difficult to discuss as was mystical union and the ineffability of God in chapter 35.

65. The vision of God is always according to the measure of man's capacity. In this life, even the most spiritually advanced can seldom sustain mystical union for more than the briefest time.

66. This vision of light can *only* be the work of God in us, since our natural faculties are utterly incapable of attaining to it by their own power. Since God is neither an object of sense perception nor of intellection, but transcends all sense and intellect, we must still both the senses and the mind to *receive* the gift of mystical knowledge.

67. Cf. Ps. 36:9: "With thee is the fountain of life, and in thy light we shall see light." In this vision God becomes all in all; for light is at once the

NOTES

"object" of the vision, and that by which we see (the medium), and indeed, the seeing eye itself (for one must be transfigured oneself into light in order to see God, and to see Him is to be united with Him and share in His glory). Nonetheless, note that the union is "without mingling": Created nature remains created, even when deified by the transforming vision.

68. 2 Cor. 12:2.

69. Palamas here lists the three faculties or levels of cognition in ascending order: sense perception (*aisthētōs*), discursive reason (*logikōs*) and the intuitive faculty (*noerōs*). Note that mystical union exceeds even the *noūs*, the contemplative or spiritual intellect.

70. A daring idea: Man himself, when he goes beyond his creatureliness to be united with God, becomes transcendent to his own self-knowledge: a "not-being (*mē on*) by transcendence", as Palamas says a little later. This phrase should not of course be pressed too far, since properly only the Divine Nature is "not-being" or "beyond being", as the source of all being.

71. The Greek Fathers are always at pains to exclude a false "angelism" in their spiritual teaching. The line is drawn firmly between uncreated and created natures, i.e., God and *all* that He has made (including angels). Man does not see God by becoming like an angel, i.e., by merely transcending his bodily nature, since even angels know God only by infused grace.

72. Cf. *Cent. Gnost.* I.54 (PG XC, 1104A) and *Ambig.*, PG XCI, 1200B.

73. Cf. *Ambig.*, *ibid.*, 1241AC.

74. An important caveat (cf. note 70, above). The divine essence must by definition always transcend created mind, even in the Age to Come, for one can never be fully united with that which is ontologically uncreated. Hence the importance of the Palamite distinction between the unknowable divine essence and the divine energies, knowable by grace.

75. Ps. Denys, *Ep.* II, PG III, 1068.

76. *Ibid.*, *de myst. theol.* V, PG III, 1948A.

77. Cf. 2 Cor. 12:2-3.

78. *Hom.* XXVIII, 19, PG XXXVI, 52B.

79. A blow at Barlaam's view that the hesychasts' claim to see the divine light is a mere product of the imagination (*phantasia*), or at best a vision of the *nous* itself as light.

80. On the concept of the spiritual paternity of Christ, see above II.iii.18 and note 38, above.

81. Mt. 13:43.

82. Cf. Rom. 8:23. The light of the Age to Come can truly be seen by anticipation (as an "earnest" of greater things to come) by the saints in this life. Although their full transfiguration, body and soul together, awaits the final Resurrection, deification can and must begin in this life.

83. Cf. Lk. 20:36.

84. A rather ambiguous sentence: It could mean either that our transfigu-

136

ration in this life is *derived* from supernatural grace, and does not naturally pertain to our essence as created (for the light infused is *un*created); or (perhaps more likely), linking the passage with what follows, the "glory" relates not to God's essence but to His energies.

85. 1 Cor. 6:17.

86. Jn. 18:21.

87. Acts 7:55–56.

88. Gk. *hesychia*. Cf. Athanasius, *Vita Antonii* 10, PG XXVI, 860AB. The reference is to the "ray of light" from heaven, which appears to banish the demons and give respite to Anthony in his struggle against the forces of evil. Because of the Fall, "inner stillness" and spiritual integration is always something that has to be fought for.

89. Cf. *de div. nom.* I.4, PG III, 592 BC.

90. Cf. Mt. 11:25; Lk. 10:21.

91. *De beat. hom.* VI (PG XLIV, 1269B).

92. *De div. nom.* VII.3, PG III, 869CD.

93. *Ibid.*, 872AB.

94. Note that Palamas does not deny the validity of "natural contemplation": the wisdom and beauty of God can indeed can be perceived in creation; but *direct* knowledge of the transcendent God in Himself must seek another, higher mode of cognition.

95. *De div. nom.*, VII. 3.

96. Cf. Maximus, *Ambig.*, PG XCI, 1076BC.

E. The uncreated glory

1. *Ambig.*, PG XCI, 1144C, cf. Cap., V. 85, PG XC, 1384D, probably recalling Gal. II. 20. The thought and expression of this and the preceding chapter of *Triads* III is very close to that of Palamas's *Letter* III to Akindynos, ed. Meyendorff, in *Theologia* XXIV, 1953, p. 579.

2. Cf. Ps. Denys, *Ep.* II, PG III, 1068–1069. The point here is that the divine energies (or light) *are* the very life of God (the "divinity") in which the saints are called to share; yet God ineffably transcends this life or divinity in His essential nature.

3. Ps. Basil, *c. Eunom.* V, PG XXIX, 772B.

4. This divine light cannot be contemplated *as* a hypostasis, that is, as an independent reality, since strictly speaking it has no essence. It can be contemplated only *in* a hypostasis, i.e., in a personal *locus*. Here Palamas has in mind the deified saints who by grace show forth in their whole persons the light that transforms them. But the energies are also "enhypostatic" in respect of the Person (*hypostasis*) of Christ. The light of Thabor does not reveal the divine essence, but the second Person of the Trinity.

As well as meaning "what exists in another hypostasis", *enhypostatic* can

NOTES

also mean "what really exists", that which is genuine or authentic, e.g., of our *real* adoption as sons by the grace of the Holy Spirit (III. i–27). The first sense of the word goes back to the christology of Leontius of Byzantium, the second to Mark the Monk.

5. In the ontological sense, i.e., as an energy pertaining to, and inherent in, the nature of the Spirit.

6. Ps. Denys, *de div. nom.* II.7, PG III, 645B.

7. That is, the Spirit transcends His self-gift, not only metaphysically, in the sense that the Cause is always ontologically prior to its energies and effects, but also as gift, since we can never (because of our human limitations as creatures) contain the divine life in its plenitude.

8. Excerpts from the Macarian writings have circulated under the names of various mediaeval writers, including Symeon Metaphrastes (tenth c.).

9. 2 Cor. 3:18.

10. Metaphrastes, *de elev. mentis* 1, PG CXXXIV, 889 = Ps. Macarius, *Logos* 48, 6–7, ed. H. Berthold, *Makarios/Symeon Reden und Briefe* II (Berlin, 1973), p. 104).

11. *De elev. mentis*, 2 *ib.*, 892AB, cf. Ps. Macarius, *ed. cit.*, p. 105). Note here Symeon's emphasis on the *eschatological* nature of sanctification: Those who receive the divine light are anticipating the resurrection-glory of the Age to Come. What now is for the most part an interior glory—though not exclusively, as in the case of Moses and several of the monastic saints of the Desert—will then be shown forth externally in the transfigured bodies of the saints.

12. 1 Thess. 4:17.

13. *De div. nom.* I.4, PG III, 592BC. The saints in heaven enjoy the same vision of the transfigured Christ as the apostles did on Thabor. The Transfiguration (so central to Eastern Christian spiritual theology) is not an isolated and ephemeral event in the life of Christ (as suggested by Barlaam), but an eternal paradigm of the vision of God, and of the transfiguration of the cosmos.

14. Cf. Rev. 21:23–24, 22:5.

15. *Ep. CI ad Cledonium*, PG XXXVII, 181AB. Gregory is referring to the Second Coming, when Christ will appear in the same glory as that in which He was revealed on Thabor. The divinity "triumphs over the flesh", not in the sense of abolishing or defeating the body, but as having overcome its corporeal opacity, rendering it a luminous vehicle of spirit.

16. The word literally means "lasting only for a day", as, for example, mayflies.

17. Cf. Plato, *Tim.* 27D, applied by Barlaam to the visions of the hesychasts (cf. *Triads* II.iii.55).

18. A phrase of Gregory Nazianzen (*vid.* note 15, above).

NOTES

19. The light of Thabor cannot be a mere created and passing symbol, because it is the glory of the changeless divinity. It is a supernatural light, visible in this life only to those whose eyes have been transformed by grace.

20. Cf. Col. 3:11; and Gregory of Nyssa, *de anima et resurr.*, PG XLVI, 104C.

21. Gregory of Nyssa, *ibid.*

22. Cf. John Chrysostom, *ad Theod. lapsum* I.11, PG XLVII, 292, on the Transfiguration, where John speaks of "beholding the King Himself, no longer in a riddle or through a mirror, but face to face" (cf. Num. 12:8 and 1 Cor. 13:12). The vision on Thabor, in all its concrete actuality, is a tangible earnest or guarantee of the reality of the unmediated and direct vision of Christ in heaven.

23. Hom. XL.6, PG XXXVI, 365A.

24. Chrysostom passage not identified.

25. That is, the light can only be the radiance of the divinity if it is itself divine, of the same nature as God. God's glory may indeed be manifested *through* creation, but it cannot itself *be* a creature or a created symbol.

26. Ps. Basil, *c. Eunom.* V, PG XXIX, 640AB, citing 1 Tim. 6:16.

27. 2 Cor. 4:6.

28. Citing the *Exaposteilarion*, a liturgical text sung in church during the Matins of the Feast (August 6). Although Christ was the sole subject of the historical Transfiguration, the divine uncreated light or energy is the common glory or energy of all Three Persons of the Trinity, and is not a property of the Son alone.

29. Last verse of the *aposticha* on Vespers for August 7.

30. Cf. *Ambig.*, PG XCI, 1376CD.

31. Cf. *ibid.*, 1165BC. Maximus means that the higher reality (the divine light) can symbolise the lower reality, i.e., the theologies which struggle to adumbrate it.

32. *Ibid.*, 1168C. This is the opposite case, a created entity used to symbolise a divine quality. The point here is that even in a case such as this, the symbol can be a reality in its own right, not something imagined or a passing phenomenon.

33. In practice, of course, most symbols of higher reality are created things, and this is why the Fathers tend to avoid describing the uncreated light as a symbol.

34. Palamas now pauses to define the only sense in which this light *is* a symbol: It is a *natural* symbol of the divinity (cf. note 5, above), connatural and coexistent with God, analogous to the inseparable relationship between the sun and its rays. Symbols *not* participating in the nature of what they symbolise either have an independent existence from that symbolised (e.g., Moses and providence), or exist only notionally, as an illustration (e.g., a conflagration as symbol of a military onslaught). Since the light of Thabor is

identical with the eternal glory of Christ, it must be a natural symbol, not a created or imaginary one, and itself truly existing and eternal. Further on this topic, *vid. infra,* chapters 19–21.

35. Zach. 5:1–2 (LXX).

36. Ezech. 9:2.

37. Cf. *supra,* Sections 10–11.

38. *Hom. in Transfig.* 12–13, PG XCIV, 564C–565A. It is not Christ who is changed into something new in the Transfiguration, but the disciples. The Transfiguration reveals the divine glory He possessed from all eternity, but which was hidden under the veils of the flesh in His Incarnation. For the apostles, these veils are momentarily drawn aside on Thabor.

39. Source not identified.

40. Cf. the third *sticheron* of the *Lite* of the Vespers of August 6.

41. An important theological point: The very assumption of our human nature by the Logos had the effect of healing and transforming it. Even in terms of Christ's humanity, then, what is shown forth at the Transfiguration is not something new at that moment; it is a revelation of the divinised human nature of Christ, which potentially may be appropriated by all who share that nature.

42. Palamas often stresses that it does not lie within our natural powers to bear the dazzling vision of God. Even those who have "purified the eyes of the heart" need a special grace to enable them to behold the uncreated light (cf. Section 17, *infra*).

43. Heb. 1:3.

44. John of Damascus, Canon II for the Feast of the Transfiguration (Ode IX, *troparion* 2).

45. *In Transfig. hom.,* VII, PG XCVII, 933C.

46. That is, the angelic hierarchy, whose members contemplate the glory of the Godhead both as it is eternally, and as incarnate in Christ.

47. *De cael. hier.,* VII.2, PG III, 20BC. This light is "theurgic" in the sense of "divinising", causing the angels to share in the life of God.

48. Heb. 8:1.

49. This passage is cited earlier, in *Triads* I.iii.29, but is not to be found in the published text of Ps. Macarius.

50. First *sticheron* of the Lauds of August 6; also, Canon of the same day, by Cosmas of Maiouma (Ode IX, *troparion* 1).

51. Cf. Section 9, above, and note 4.

52. The point of this terminological paragraph is that the divine light or energy is neither an independent reality apart from the three divine Persons, nor something temporary and fleeting, but exists permanently as an outgoing power *in* God. Like personal attributes, the energies must have a personal (or hypostatic) *locus*—by nature, they inhere in the Divine Persons, by grace, in us; and it is this that is meant by the term *"en*hypostatic".

NOTES

53. A reference to the christological decree of the Council of Chalcedon (451). The divine light does not *naturally* pertain to our created nature, but even in the case of unfallen Adam, is always a gift of God. So the light can be only the natural symbol of Christ's *divine* nature.

54. Acts 1:4.

55. *Kontakion* of the Feast of the Transfiguration.

56. *Hom. in Transfig.* 12, PG XCVI, 564B.

57. Cf. *Cent. gnost.* I.48, PG XC, 1100D—an especially important text for Palamas's theology, giving patristic authority for his doctrine that divine energies are permanently related to the divine essence, and are therefore eternal and uncreated. The other "realities contemplated around God" (*ta peri theoŭ*) would include such divine attributes as goodness, justice and providence.

58. God in His essence is unitary and utterly simple, yet ineffably contains multiplicity within Himself: primarily, the triunity of Persons, but also the plenitude of divine attributes, powers and energies. It is only on the plane of limited human logic that the existence of the One and the Many in God presents an intellectual problem.

59. *Kathisma* after the *polyeleon* of Matins on August 6.

60. *Ambig.*, PG XCI, 1165D.

61. Because there is no continuity or affinity of nature between symbol and object, as in the case of natural symbols. Since light and heat are naturally derived from fire, or energy from essence, we can say that a single entity is under consideration, and in a sense, the light is its own symbol.

62. The image of fire is borrowed from Ps. Denys, *de cael. hier.* XV.2, PG III, 326Dff.

63. The analogy of the sun's light is an appropriate one, since it is not only the object of vision, but that medium *in* which all vision takes place. Similarly, there can be no vision of God without participation in His light and life. The gift of divine light is what enables man to see divine realities (including itself) at all.

64. A Dionysian periphrasis for "angels". Not even the angels can know the divine mysteries fully; how much less can men?

65. On this point (that man must transcend his natural powers by grace to see the divine light), see notes 42 and 63, above.

66. *Hom. in Transfig.* 12, PG XCVI, 564C.

67. It is important to note that the vision of God is not simply an *interior* experience, but according to Palamas, involves also the *bodily* eyes, transfigured by grace. The whole man is the subject of divinisation, not just the intellectual or spiritual principle.

68. Cf. text of Barlaam cited above, Section 10.

69. *Hom. in Transfig.* 10, PG XCVI, 561D.

70. 1 Thess. 4:17.

71. Damascene, *ibid.*, 15–16 (*ibid.* 569AB).

141

NOTES

72. *Ibid.*, 7, 557C.

73. Cf. *de div. nom.* I.4, PG III, 592BC. If the light of Thabor is one with the light of eternity, it must be that it is not "sensible", i.e., accessible to sense perception as such, and so cannot be a created symbol, as Barlaam maintains.

74. According to the Platonists, something perceptible through the senses is necessarily ontologically inferior to a reality knowable through the mind alone. If, then, the light of Thabor is "sensible", it is also inferior to "intelligible" things and to our own intellection.

75. Cf. *Hom. in Transfig.* VII, PG XCVII, 949C.

76. *Ekstasis* in patristic theology is primarily a matter of "going out" of oneself under the impetus of divine love; but there is also the pejorative sense (as here) of being "out of one's mind", as a result of demonic possession.

77. Third *sticheron* of the *aposticha* of the Vespers of August 6.

78. *De div. nom.* II.7, PG III, 645A.

79. A major statement: It is central to Palamas's case that the energies are not to be confounded with the essence of God; even though the energies are divine and essential (i.e., pertaining to God's essence), yet the essence transcends them as Source, and gathers them all into unity. Following Ps. Denys (cf. *de div. nom.* V.2, *ibid.*, 916C), Palamas is prepared to call them collectively "divinity"; but the Godhead in its utterly transcendent ground of being is "more-than-God" and "superessential". We can participate in the deifying energies, but the essence remains permanently inaccessible to created beings ("imparticipable").

80. Barlaam refuses to accept the Dionysian distinctions explained in note 79. For him, what possesses the apophatic attributes of God (immaterial, unchangeable, etc.) can only be the divine essence. Since, as Palamas admits, the energies are not to be identified with the essence, they must be created effects of God.

81. Barlaam concludes that Palamas is ditheistic in positing *two* principles in God, the superessential essence and the divine energies. But (as Palamas explains) since the divine light is not "hypostatic" or individuated, it cannot be a second God.

82. Without energies, God would simply be an inert transcendent deity, not a providential creator. On the question of the simple and the composite in God, see note 58, above.

83. *Ad Marinum*, PG. XCI, 268D.

84. In other words, the energies would not be God if they did not share with the essence of God the divine attributes.

85. The Messalian error in question is the view that sanctification is a work of human effort, unaided by grace. It represents a Pelagian account of the spiritual life: Man deifies himself by his own powers.

86. Maximus, *Quaest. ad Thal.* 22, PG XC, 342A, paraphrased in *Cap.* I 75, PG XC, 1209C.

NOTES

87. Palamas is here following the thought of St. Maximus on being and movement. On the purely natural plane, perfection consists in becoming what one is, realising all the inherent possibilities of one's nature. (Cf. H. Urs von Balthasar, *Liturgie Cosmique*, Paris, 1947, pp. 94f.).

88. In fact, true experiential knowledge of God and union with Him always involves *ekstasis* ("going out from oneself") and self-transcendence on the part of man. It is something quite beyond his natural powers, though he must *cooperate* with God in this work (the Eastern doctrine of *synergy*) and predispose himself for union with God by practice of the virtues.

89. *Ambig.*, PG XCI, 1240A.

90. *Ibid.*, 1076C.

91. Cf. *ibid.*, 1088B, 1320B. But the analogy should not be pressed too far, even though "it" (next sentence) would seem to refer to the body. The Holy Spirit does not take the place of the soul in the union, but reforms the whole man into the image of the Son ("the adoption as sons", *hyiothesia*).

92. Cf. Basil, *Ep.* 2.4, PG XXXII, 229B.

93. *De Spir. Sancto*, 16, 40, PG XXXII, 141AB.

94. Matt. 13:43.

95. Cf. Ps. 81 (82); 1.

96. Unidentified quotation.

97. Prov. 13:9.

98. Col. 1:12.

99. Num. 12:8; cf. *Triads* II.iii.59.

100. In the sense that the divine life finds its personal *locus* in each of those being sanctified.

101. Maximus, *Ad Thalas.* 61, PG XC, 636C; also *Scholion* 16, *ibid.* 644C.

102. Cf. *de cael. hier.* III.2, PG III, 165A. One might paraphrase, "a transcendent and divinising glory".

103. *Ep.* II, PG III, 1068–1069.

104. Palamas is here interpreting, not actually quoting, Ps. Denys.

105. Num. 12:8.

106. Tit. 3:6.

107. In other words, although God does indeed come down to meet us in His fulness in the divine energies (and this is "God" properly speaking, "thearchy", "divinity" or "deification"), He remains permanently unknowable and inaccessible ("transcends the thearchy") in the inexhaustible mystery of His being (the "superessential essence"). We must beware of supposing that even the totality of all that we can ever know of God is an *exhaustive* knowledge. God unites Himself completely with man in the mystical union, yet remains ineffably *other*, even in that union. Hence the importance of the Palamite distinction between essence and energies in God, to denote a God Who is at once well known and yet unknown.

108. That is, Barlaam. The argument now reverts to the problem of

whether deification is a natural perfection or a supernatural grace (cf. chapters 26–27, above).

109. Jn. 1:13.

110. Jn. 3:16.

111. Jn. 1:12.

112. A curious idea: Intellectual maturation is primarily a physical matter.

113. That is, deification is a state that goes *beyond* that perfection natural to a created rational being. Even were one to realise fully all one's physical and intellectual potential—and this itself would require divine help—one would still not share in the life of God. Only a power greater than man can divinise us, and so the deifying energies must be divine.

114. See note 91, above (cf. chapters 9, 18, above).

115. Cf. *Ambig.*, PG XCI, 1140A, 1144C.

116. A bold thought: The deified saints (while remaining creatures) come to share by grace in the *un*created nature of God, and are thus to be described by the apophatic adjectives appropriate to the *divine* transcendence.

117. If, that is, the energies pertain to the very essence of God, rather than being (as claimed by Barlaam) created powers (cf. the Western Scholastic doctrine of the created effects of grace in us). But if God is knowable only through *created* grace, then the direct and personal union of God and man becomes impossible.

118. A phrase borrowed from Ps. Denys (cf. note 47 above, and *Triads* I. iii. 23), for whom "theurgic" and "deifying" grace would seem to have approximately the same meaning.

119. This represents a further refinement of Eastern Trinitarian theology: Since the divine essence transcends all names—even the name "God"—the divine names (goodness, wisdom, etc.) relate to the energies common to the Three Persons.

120. The Greek Fathers frequently affirm that the words God (*theos*) or Godhead (*theotēs*) denote an energy of God, and not the essence; by rather dubious etymology, they relate the Greek root *the* to divine activities such as seeing, burning or even running. *Vid.*, e.g., Basil, *Ep.* CXXXIX. 8, PG XXXII, 696; Gregory of Nyssa, *Ep. ad Ablabium*, PG, XLV, 121D–124A (ed. W. Jaeger [Leiden, 1958], pp. 44–45; Gregory Nazianzen, *Hom.* XXX.18, PG XXXVI, 128A; Ps. Denys, *de div. nom.* XII.2, PG III, 969C.

121. Were there no intermediate mode of being between essence and attributes, God would transcend only His own virtues. But in fact, He is more transcendent even than this, going beyond even the "divinity" (the energies collectively) from which the attributes derive, and so can be called "more-than-God" (*hypertheos*), as Ps. Denys teaches.

122. But in the end, the divine energies are to be known experientially, not intellectually, for truth comes to us through the inner working of the

NOTES

Holy Spirit, not by speculation *about* the nature of God. Palamas's often highly technical defence of the energies doctrine is geared precisely towards the vindication of the primacy of experience in religious knowledge, and of the possibility of a direct personal relationship with God even in this life.

123. Probably a citation not from Basil but from Chrysostom (*In Is.* I, PG LVI, 14).

124. In the absence of direct personal illumination, the way of humility is to trust those saints who *have* had direct experience of divine things. Theologising not based on experience will almost certainly result in error.

125. A good example of patristic apophatic reserve. Only the necessity of defending the truth against the attacks of heretics impels the theologian to probe and define matters that ultimately transcend all thought and language. Those who have received the grace.

126. This is why men and angels can know God only in a state of *ecstasis* or self-transcendence.

127. Such hypostatic union uniquely took place in the Incarnation, and this was itself a miracle of grace.

The union effected by grace between God and a saint is a union without confusion of two distinct persons (or hypostases); whereas in the Incarnation, the Logos unites Himself with the whole human nature (not only to an individual) and in this unique union becomes Himself the hypostasis of Jesus Christ. Thus we may say that divinised men are united to God by grace, not hypostatically.

128. Gregory Nazianzen, *Hom.* XXX, 21, PG XXXVI, 132B.

129. This does not, of course, mean that essence and energy in God are identical (for the one transcends the other), but that the *same* energy that eternally exists in God is made present in the saints, and shown forth in the quality of their lives. (Cf. Maximus, *Ambig.*, PG XCI, 1076BC: "so that there is in all respects one and the same energy of God and of those worthy of Him".)

130. Col. 2:19.

131. Cf. Andrew of Crete, *hom. VII in Transfig.* PG XCVII, and also an unidentified text of Basil, cited *apud Triads* I.iii.29.

132. 1 Cor. 15:20 and 23: Christ as "firstfruits of salvation", in whose humanity deification is first realised.

133. *De Spir. Sancto* 26, ed. Pruche, p. 226. The grace of divinisation subsists in the saint as the creative power in the artist, for it is essentially a communication of living power from God to man, creating *by grace* a personal relationship with God. Art, on the other hand, is naturally and automatically inherent in the work of art, which remains in itself an inert object.

134. Man is thus able to create as one recreated in the image of the Supreme Artist, since both share the same creative energy. The works of the saint are in a real sense the works of the Holy Spirit.

135. Mt. 10:20.

NOTES

136. Num. 11:17.

137. Acts 19:6.

138. Ps. Basil, *c. Eun.* 5, PG XXIX, 772D.

139. *De Spir. Sancto* 26, ed. Pruche, pp. 226–227.

140. The divine energy of the Spirit is fully present to all, yet in the measure to which each is able to receive it.

141. Cf. Lk. 1:35.

142. Col. 2:9.

143. Jn. 1:16.

144. Cf. Wis. 1:7.

145. That is, deifying grace needs a human agent in order to become visible in the world, both illuminating the saints and, through their transfigured souls and bodies, becoming knowable to others.

146. A favourite text of Palamas, and attributed by him to St. Basil (in an unpublished patristic anthology [= Ms. *Paris. gr.* 970, f. 325ᵛ] compiled by him or one of his disciples during the controversy with Barlaam).

147. Mt. 13:43.

148. Source unidentified; but parallel ideas in Gregory of Nyssa, *In Hex.*, PG XLIV, 88. The image of the mirror is also very common in Gregory of Nyssa.

149. Cf. Jn. 1:5.

150. Cf. Mt. 5:14.

151. *Ambig.*, PG XCI, 1144C; cf. *Cap.* V.85, PG XC, 1384D. The idea rests on Gal. 2:20.

152. For the distinction between "natural" and ordinary symbols, see chapters 13–14, 19–20, and the notes relating to these chapters.

153. To attain to the vision of the uncreated light is to see "light by light"; for only the light itself can transform the eyes of him who seeks to see.

154. Dispassion, humility, joy, love of God are all in some measure prerequisites of the vision of God; but these virtues are increased and perfected by the vision itself.

155. Cf. citations of Barlaam *apud* chapters 11 and 25, above.

156. Cf. *de myst. theol.* I.1, PG III, 997B.

157. That is, the natural faculties of sense perception and intellection are not abolished (or even necessarily suspended) by the vision, but *transcended* (hence the terms "sense-above-sense", "mind-above-mind"). Sometimes, indeed, the contemplative is so overcome with wonder as to become oblivious of his surroundings, but at others, a heightened awareness of God can coexist with the usual operations of the senses and the mind (cf. Maximus, *Cent. gnost.* 11.83, PG XCI, 1164B: "The establishment of the mind of Christ in us does not involve depriving us of our intellectual faculties").

158. Acts 2:15.

159. Macarius-Symeon, *de libert.mentis* 23, PG XXXIV, 957B.

NOTES

160. 2 Cor. 3:17.

161. 1 Cor. 1:30.

162. Ps. Basil, *c. Eun.* 5, PG XXIX, 769B; cf. Gen. 18:27.

163. Unidentified citation.

164. Lk. 21:15.

165. Mt. 10:20.

F. Essence and energies in God

1. Even though it might be possible for a philosopher to conceive of a transcendent One or First Essence without attributes, the data of revelation make it impossible for the Christian God not to be creator and redeemer. Hence, the divine attributes must always have subsisted in the essence, since by nature God is changeless.

2. On the spiritual senses, see Section B, note 33, above. The soul possesses a single *sensorium* (sometimes called by the Fathers *to pathētikon*, or the passionate part of the soul), but it contains without division the various spiritual faculties of sight, touch, etc.

3. Such powers as providence and creativity are present too in angels and men to various degrees, but their powers are necessarily created and contingent, as are their virtues.

4. That is, God's powers, energies and attributes are also uncreated.

5. Palamas is using the word "works" (*erga*) here, not in the sense of God's creation (as in the O.T.) but in the sense of those powers such as providence and prescience that enabled Him eternally to foresee and foreplan His creation. By extension, "works" also refers to the pre-existence of creation as an idea in the mind of God (as "predeterminations").

6. That is, the Arian heretics.

7. Cf. 1 Cor. 2:7.

8. There seems to be little precise distinction in our text between the terms "power", "work", "virtue", as descriptions of God's providence, prescience and similar faculties. The virtues are the divine attributes or qualities, collectively referred to as *ta peri autov* (*lit.*, "the things that surround Him").

9. *Sc.*, created essence.

10. *Cent. gnost.* 1.48 PG XC, 1100D, cited above, III.i.19.

11. *Ibid.*, 50 (*ib.*, 1101B).

12. *loc. cit.*

13. Man, as created in the image of God, possesses a natural kinship to God (albeit this has been eroded by the Fall). But our virtues, though participating in and mirroring more or less the eternal attributes of God (e.g., good, wise, etc.) are not *identical* with those divine attributes: They are derivative, and have a beginning in time.

NOTES

14. Cf. *ibid*. 48, PG XC, 1100CD.

15. Note the distinction drawn here between works of God that do have a beginning in time and those that do not (cf. note 5, above).

16. *Ibid*. (1000D–1101A).

17. By stripping the spiritual intellect of all contingent concepts in a state of purity of heart, it may be possible through grace for the mind to transcend itself, and gain some apperception of the God Who is beyond essence. This is the apophatic way of the Christian East—seen not as a method of intellectual abstraction, but as a mode of spiritual initiation.

18. *Ibid*. 49 (*ib*., 1101A): God's essence and His virtues are both unoriginate, yet God infinitely transcends these uncreated energies or powers. Although God has revealed Himself *as* goodness, love, etc., our sense of His utter transcendence (beyond all names and qualities in essence) must forbid us simply to *identify* essence and attributes/virtues/energies in God.

19. Cf. *Ep*. CXXXIX, 6–7, PG XXXII, 692–696. An essence, unknowable in itself, is known by its energies or operations *ad extra*. By observing these "works", one may rise to some apprehension of the character of the nature that produces them. "Natural" energy here must be taken in the metaphysical sense of that activity or those characteristics which pertain to each nature, and which are part of its concrete actuality.

20. It is by reason of His transcendence that God in some ineffable way can be wholly present in each of His many attributes or energies, without prejudice to His absolute simplicity and unity. For this reason, we can truly call God wise, just (and all the other adjectives revealed in the cataphatic theology), without supposing that these different qualities are discrete metaphysical entities (like the Platonic "ideas"); or that any (or indeed all) exhaust the reality of the divine mystery.

21. Palamas now concedes that there are *some* energies that had a beginning, at least in their external operations, though not as pre-existent in the mind of God. Thus, for instance, God's creative energy became effective only when creation and time simultaneously began, yet God always possessed a creative power and purpose.

22. *Vid*. above, 4.

23. Gen. 2:3.

24. Probably a reference to *c. Eun*. I.8, PG XXIX, 528B. The divine prescience (*prognōsis*) has an "end" in the sense that time comes to an end in eternity, and there are no events or developments in the Age to Come for God to foresee.

Palamas's thought on the uncreated energies that are not unoriginate may be summarised as follows: All are functions of God's temporal "economy", some (like the creative power) only being activated when time begins, others (like prescience) no longer operating when this world passes away.

NOTES

This temporary nature of certain energies is a further argument for distinguishing between essence and energies in God.

25. *Cent. gnost.* I.7 (PG XC, 1085B); I.49 (*ibid.*, 1101A); *Ad Thal.*, LXIII, PG XC, 673D, etc.

26. That is, the energies are the divine immanence in the cosmos. But this omnipresence is only a *mode* of God's existence, not His being itself.

27. This passage is to be found in the patristic anthology forming an appendix to Maximus's *Opusc. theol.* PG XCI, 281BC.

28. *C. Eun.* I.8, PG XXIX, 528B.

29. *Cent. gnost.* I.48, PG XC, 1100D. The divine qualities, inherent in God, are of necessity ontologically prior to all in the created realm, even "nonbeing" (which is simply the negative aspect of the existence of anything contingent).

30. "In Him"/"around Him": prepositional synonyms for essence and energies.

31. This pseudo-etymology is discussed above, Section E, note 120. Cf. Gregory Nazianzen, *Hom.* XXX.18, PG XXXVI, 128A; Gregory of Nyssa, *Ad Ablab.*, PG XLV, 121D–124A (ed. W. Jaeger (Leiden, 1958), pp. 44–45).

32. Cf. Ps. Denys, *de div. nom.* XI.6, PG III, 956A.

33. The transcendence of essence over energies is as *Cause*; yet this priority is ontological not temporary, for God was never without His energies. Cause eternally presupposes effects, just as the Father's paternity eternally presupposes the existence of His Son—yet the Father remains the "*font* of the Godhead" (*Pēgē tēs theotētos*), in John Damascene's phrase.

34. *De div. nom.* II.7, PG III, 645A. God is said to transcend even essence in the sense that He goes beyond every positive concept whatsoever we may have concerning Him (hence Denys's peculiar "supereminent" (*hyper*) epithets: "superluminous", "more-than-God", etc.). Nonetheless, one must recall that Palamas (and the Fathers in general) regularly use the word "essence" for that which is ultimately transcendent in God's ground of being.

35. In this chapter, however, Palamas is using "essence" to describe one of the divine energies, that which creates substance in the cosmos. The polemical aim of this usage is to convict Barlaam of inconsistency in accepting this one energy as without beginning, but not any of the others.

36. Ex. 3:14.

37. Cf. Gregory Nazianzen, *Hom.* XLV. 3, PG XXXVI, 625C, and Ps. Denys, *de div. nom.* V.4, PG III, 817C. That is, God is not one being (or essence) among many in the world, but as the universal Source of being, "transcends being in essence".

38. Even the name "God" cannot be used of the Deity without qualification, for deified saints are also called (derivatively) "gods by grace" in patristic tradition. They participate in the divine nature by grace, not by nature;

NOTES

and remain always creatures, dependent on the Creator for their life in Him.

39. Cf. Maximus, *Ambig.*, PG XCI, 1144C. Note the daring phrase "unoriginate and uncreated by grace": humanly speaking, a contradiction in terms! Creatures can never *become* uncreated, though they can come to share in the nature of the uncreated God.

40. *De div. nom.* XI.6, PG III, 953D–956A. The energies ("providential powers") form the essential link between the divine essence (in which none can participate) and creatures. The latter truly live only to the extent to which they participate in the divine energies.

41. That is, Ps. Denys.

42. Barlaam, in his anxiety to drive as hard a wedge as possible between the utterly transcendent Deity and all else, here misinterprets Denys to mean that even "divinity" and deification are created powers of God.

43. *Hom.* XXVIII. 31, PG XXXVI, 72C.

44. Because the vision of God is a mode of participation in Him (*sc.*, in His energies, cf. note 40, above).

45. *De div. nom.* IV.8, PG III, 704D. These "illuminations" (*ellampseis*) must be distinct from the essence, since Denys states that the angels are united to them, whereas no creature can be united to the divine essence.

46. Moreover, the essence is simple and unitary and indivisible, whereas the energies are experienced as manifold and varied, and visible as the uncreated light of Thabor.

47. Heb. 2:4.

48. But Palamas is careful to stress that although the saints can see and be united by grace to the divine light, this light remains transcendent to all *natural* sense perception and intellection.

49. Cited in note 43, above.

50. *Loc. cit.*

51. This idea is further developed in section 16 below.

52. Ps. Basil, *c. Eun.*, 5, PG XXIX, 769B; cf. Gen. 18:27.

53. *De div. nom.* IV.8, PG III, 704D.

54. That is, even the angels who never fell from grace contemplate the divine glory not by their natural powers but at the prompting and help of God.

55. That is, the Devil.

56. If the power of contemplation were inherent in the nature of an angel, then even the fallen angels (the demons) would still retain this power, just as they have retained their faculty of reason.

57. Mk. 1:24.

58. Mk. 1:24; Lk. 4:41.

59. *Hom.* XLV.27, PG XXXVI, 661A.

60. Cf. Isa. 10:12.

61. Because the uncreated light is transcendent and suprarational, it is

both unknowable to the spiritually immature, and incapable of remaining with anyone who inclines towards evil.

62. This energy is divine because it *is* the Holy Spirit at work, illuminating and sanctifying the elect.

63. *Triads* III.ii.4, where he accuses Barlaam of the errors of the extreme Arian Eunomius, who taught that both the Son and the Spirit were creatures.

64. Cf. *de div. nom.* XI.6, PG III, 953B. Much in this paragraph turns on the play on the words *hypostasis* and *hypostēsai;* from the verb *hyphistemi* to establish, *lit.*, place/set under). Needless to say, this is very hard to convey in translation.

Clearly Barlaam's citation from Ps. Denys has caused real diffculties for Palamas. He strives to show that Denys used the word "established" of the powers, not in the sense of creating them from nothing; but in the sense that the Cappadocian Fathers speak of the Father "establishing" the Son and Spirit, as sources of their hypostases (or Persons).

65. Job 38:28.

66. *C. Eun.* II.23, PG XXIX, 624A This text of St. Basil will later (in 1356–1357) serve as the topic of a special treatise by Palamas during his polemics with Nicephorous Gregoras (see J. Meyendorff, *Introduction a l'étude de Grégoire Palamas* [Paris, 1959], p. 378).

67. Ps. 32 (33):6.

68. *Hom. in Ps. XXXII,* 4, PG XXIX, 333B.

69. Basil *Ep.* XXXVIII.4, PG XXXII, 329C.

70. *Hom.* 20, 6, PG XXXV, 1072c; 42, 16, PG XXXVI, 477AB, etc.

71. If Barlaam is going to misuse the Dionysian phrase to prove that the divine energies are created, by the same token, he might as well understand Basil and the Gregories' use of the verb *hypostēsai* in an Arian sense, and claim the Son and the Spirit are creatures too.

72. *De div. nom.* XI.6, PG III, 956AB.

73. Cf. *Cent. gnost.* I.48, PG XC, 1100CD. "That in which they participate" means the divine energies.

74. That is, a man may be elevated by God to enjoy angelic contemplation, but he does not cease to be a man, for all that. The contemplative life is sometimes described as an "angelic life"in Eastern monastic sources, in the sense of that mode of Christian living most detached from worldly ties.

75. God (the "Master of Necessities") is not bound by the hierarchical order He has established among angels and men. Although angels do often mediate between God and men, God is quite capable of establishing a direct personal relationship with those men He has chosen. Palamas goes on to cite examples from the O.T. of God appearing to the Patriarchs and Prophets without intermediary; and then brings forward the appearance of God the Son in the flesh. Thus, Palamas gives a decisive biblical and christological corrective to the hierarchical system of Ps. Denys, who considered the media-

NOTES

tion of angels as an absolute condition of communion with God (cf. J. Meyendorff, "Notes sur l'influence dionysienne en Orient," *Studia Patristica* II [Berlin, 1957], pp. 547–552).

76. Ex. 3:14–15.

77. *C. Eun.* II.18, PG XXIX, 609B.

78. Ex. 33:11.

79. Gen. 22:16.

80. Heb. 6:13.

81. Isa. 63:9.

82. Cf. Jn. 16:13.

83. Cf. Rom. 5:6.

84. Acts 7:55–56.

85. Cf. Ps. 35 (36):10.

86. *Hom. in S. Stephanum*, PG XLVI, 716D–717A.

87. Jn. 1:18.

88. Stephen's vision was not an act of the intellect (for the untransformed mind cannot know God directly), but a direct vision of the uncreated glory of the Trinity through the grace of the Spirit.

89. Cf. Gregory of Nyssa, *In S. Steph.*, PG XLVI, 717B.

90. Barlaam now reverts to his view that only the divine essence is uncreated and without beginning, and therefore either essence and energy in God are identical realities, or the energies are created things.

91. Cf. *Ep. ad Nicandr.*, PG XCI, 96B; *Opusc. theol. et pol., ib.,* 200C, 205AC; *Disput. cum Pyrrho, ibid.,* 340D.

92. Every essence must possess natural energies, and these must be of the same nature as the essence. If, then, the divine energies are created entities, God Himself must be created!

93. According to orthodox christology (evolved in its final form only after the Monothelite controversy in the time of St. Maximus), there subsist in the single Person of Christ two natures and two wills or energies (human and divine).

94. A polemical exaggeration. Since the divine will in Christ is an energy of God, Barlaam (by claiming the energies are created) is in fact suggesting that Christ originally had only one will and energy (the human), and therefore only one nature. Thus Barlaam is slipping into the errors of the ancient Monophysite and Monothelite heretics, who believed (respectively) that there was only one nature and one will in Christ. However, he is worse than they, who claimed the single nature/will in Christ was *divine*, whereas Barlaam affirms that it is human and created.

95. Cf. *Ep.* II, PG III, 1068–1069. This point—the transcendence of the superessential God over His energies or "divinity"—has been treated often before, e.g., III.ii.23 and note 79, Section E; *ibid.* 29 and note 107.

96. Cf. *de char.*, III.25, PG XC, 1024C.

NOTES

97. The saints do indeed "participate in the divine nature", as 2 Peter 1:4 says, but according to the energies, never according to the essence. "Nature" is here being used in a less precise sense than in the text of Palamas. If they participated according to the essence, the ontological distinction between God and man, between uncreated and created natures, would be abolished.

98. *Cent. gnost.* I.48, PG XC, 1100D.

99. Heb. 7:3.

100. Cf. Maximus, *Ambig.*, PG XCI, 1144BC; and *Cap.* V.85, PG XC, 1384D.

101. That is, the uncreated energies, through which God created all things.

102. Cf. the *Kathisma* after the *polyeleon* for Matins on August 6.

103. Cf. 3rd *Sticheron* of the *Lite* of Vespers of August 6.

104. At Pentecost, and thereafter in the fulness of their ecclesiastical experience; for the vision of Thabor is but an anticipation of the fellowship of God with believers in the sacramental life of the Church (cf. *Triads* I.iii.38).

105. *Vid. supra*, III.i.24 and note 67, Section E.

106. *Hom. in Transfig.*, 12, PG XCVI, 564C.

107. *De div. nom*, I.4, PG III, 592BC.

108. Maximus, *Cent. gnost.* II.4, PG. XC, 1128A. The man worthy to contemplate God sees in the Logos the pre-existent *logoi* or inner principles of created things (this is "natural theology" in the patristic sense, the knowledge of creation in God—not (as in the West) the deduction of divine attributes from God's works in creation).

109. Maximus, *Myst.* 5, PG XCI, 681B.

110. Cf., Section A, note 27, and Section B, note 32. God grants new spiritual senses and a "higher mind" to those deemed worthy to see and know Him.

111. Because the hesychasts claimed to be able to see the uncreated light with the (transformed) eyes of the body, Barlaam concludes that what can be perceived by the senses must be a sensible (and therefore created) reality.

112. That is, the energies that proceed from the essence are intrinsic to God's being, His natural attributes, and not discrete created entities having an existence separate from God.

113. If God is known from His effects, Barlaam says, just as all natures are known (e.g., the sun is known from its heat and light), in this respect He is no different from created natures. (But, in fact, Barlaam would not accept the first premise of this statement, and does not believe God can be known directly, as is the sun from its rays.) Palamas points out that it is not valid to argue by analogy from created and sensible natures to the uncreated Nature, imperceptible to our natural senses.

114. Cf. citation of Barlaam *apud Triads* II.i.11.

NOTES

115. Gregory of Nyssa, *de anim. et resurr.*, PG XLVI, 104C.

116. That is, in the Age to Come, in heaven.

117. Barlaam is citing Gregory Nazianzen ("the Theologian"), *Hom.* XLV.3, PG XXXVI, 625C–628A.

118. Nazianzen, *ibid.* (*ib.* 628A).

119. According to Barlaam, God can only be known *in*directly, by the intellectual contemplation of His works in nature. Palamas agrees that God may lead us up to knowledge of Himself from this point, but only so that we may come to desire that higher knowledge inaccessible to the natural mind, but accessible by grace. The purification of the mind is only the first (and easiest) step in the ascent to God; a radical total conversion, moral and spiritual, is required before a man is ready to receive the vision of the uncreated light ("by a divine power").

120. Nazianzen, *loc. cit.* (n. 117).

121. Palamas in this chapter establishes from Maximus that the grace of direct knowledge of God *is* the deifying light of Thabor, by which God unites the saints to Himself.

122. *Ambig.*, PG XCI, 1088C.

123. *Ibid.*

124. *Ibid.*

125. *Ep.* II, PG III, 1068–1069.

126. *De div. nom.* II.10, PG III, 648D.

127. God can be called "nonbeing by transcendence" in the sense that He is beyond being ("superessential") as the Source of all being.

128. Jn. 17:21.

129. Ps. Denys, *de myst. theol.* 5, PG III, 1048B *et passim.*

130. Maximus, *Cent. gnost.* I.7, PG XC, 1085B and I.9, *ib.*, 1101A; *Ad Thal.* 63, *ibid.*, 673D.

131. Barlaam takes a very literalistic and arid view of dispassion (*apatheia*) as a necessary prerequisite for the vision of God. Since his model of knowledge of God is essentially intellectualist he believes all the passions (good or bad) must be mortified in order to attain to knowledge (cf. citation of Barlaam above, *Triads* II.ii.23). Palamas replies that the passionate part of the soul must be transformed not suppressed. While it is true that the perverted passions do "close up the eye of the soul" and harden the heart against communion with God, the soul's natural impulses of love and fervour may and must be converted to devotion to God and our neighbours. For it is through love that we attain to friendship with God, and are found worthy of the unmediated vision of His uncreated glory.

132. Mt. 27:40.

Index to Foreword, Preface,
and Introduction

INDEX

Communion with God (divinity), 8, 9, 14, 17, 18, 19–20

Constantinople, xi, 5, 6, 8, 9

Constantinople, Synod of, (1368), xi, 8

Contemplation, 1, 12, 14, 15

1 Corinthians: 6:19, 16; mentioned, 12

Deification, 12, 17, 18, 19

Denys the Areopagite, St. *See* Dionysius the Areopagite, St.

Diadochus of Photice, St., 4

Dionysius the Areopagite, St. (Pseudo Dionysius), ix, 12, 13, 21

Divinisation. *See* Deification

Dostoevsky, Fyodor, xiii

Eastern Church, xii

Energies of God, the, xii, 7, 9, 14, 18–19, 20–22

Ephesians: 3:6, 19

Esphigmenou, the monastery of, 6

Essence of God, the, xi, 4, 7, 9, 14–15, 18, 20–22

Eternity, 18

Eucharist, the, 16, 18

Euchites, 4. *See also* Messalian movement, the

Evagrius Ponticus; Christocentrism of, 2–4; and hesychasm, 2; and Neoplatonism, 2–3; and prayer, 2–3, 4, 15, 116n26; mentioned, 114n4, 114n5

Existentialism, xii–xiii

Exodus, the Book of: 3:14, 21

Fall, the, 2

Fathers, the Church. *See* Church Fathers, the

Filioque, the, 6

First Vatican Council, the, xii

God: acts (actions) of, 13, 16; apophatic approach to, 14, 17; as beyond knowledge, 13; as beyond unknowing, 13; the cloud surrounding, 14; communion with, 8, 9, 14, 18, 20, 21–22; in the darkness of unknowing, 14; the

divine presence of, 1, 4, 13, 14, 17; the energies of, xii, 7, 9, 19–22; the essence of, xi, 4, 7, 9, 14–15, 18, 20–22; and existentialism, xii; fellowship with, 18; the grace of, 3, 9, 13; immanence of, 22; incarnated, 3; as inexhaustible, 18; the Kingdom of, 13; as Light, 17–18; the Living, 1, 21; man created in image of, 14, 18; manifestation of, 17; and man's body, 16; man's contemplation of, 13–14; man's knowledge of, 6, 8–9, 12–15; man's love of, 14; man's personal experience of, 1, 4, 14, 20; man's vision of, 12–13, 17, 20; and Moses, 14, 21; the Name of, 4; the nature of, 19; and negative theology, 13; the Nicene doctrine of, xi; as the "One Who Is," 21; operation of, xi; and prayer, 2–3; reveals Himself, 15; the simplicity of, 116n38; the Son of, 19; and the soul of man, 16; the Spirit of, 14; the transcendence of, xii, 7, 13–15, 17, 18, 20–22; as the Unknowable, 15

Grace: created, 9, 22; nature and, 13, 18

Granfield, P., 114n9

Great Lavra, the, 5, 6

Gregoras, Nicephorus, 7, 9, 10

Gregory of Nyssa, St., 14, 17

Gregory of Palamas, St. *See* Palamas, St. Gregory

Haghiorite, St. Nicodemus the, 114n10

Hagiography, 6

Hausherr, Irénée, xiii

Heart, the: and the divine Presence, 17; as instrument of the Holy Spirit, 16; and prayer, 15; mentioned, 114n7

Hesychasm (Hesychasts): Barlaam and, 4, 6, 8–10, 12–13, 16, 20–22; and the Messalians, 4, 20; and the Orthodox Church, xi, xii, 4; Palamas and, 5–7, 8–10, 17, 20–22; the tradition of, 1–5, 114n10

Holy Spirit, the: the body as temple of, 16; the heart as the instrument of, 16; the laws of, 3; the New

156

INDEX

Covenant in, 3; the power of, 3; and the spirit of man, 18

Humanism, secular, 12

Hunter, Daniel Honorius, xii

Hypostasis: hypostatic light, 17; hypostatic union, 18–19, 22; mentioned, 14

Illumination, 12–13, 17, 19, 21

Incarnation, the 3, 18

Irenaeus of Lyons, St., 18

Isaiah: 54:13, 3

Isidore, 7

Italos, John, 11

Jesus Christ: the body of, 18, 19, 22; in the Bread and Wine of Eucharist, 19; communion in, 21; deification of man in, 8, 17–20; the divinity of, 19; the humanity of, 19; the "Jesus Prayer," 3–5, 8; the Kingdom of God revealed in, 13; life in, 20; as the Logos, 18, 19; and the Messianic age, 20; as Second Person of the Trinity, 18; as Son of God, 19; the Transfiguration of, 17, 19–20; the uncreated glory of, 17–20

John, the Gospel of: 6:45, 3

John Calecus, 7

John Cantacuzenos, the Grand Domesticus, 7

John Climacus, St., 4

John of Damascus, St., 17

Jugie, Martin, xi, 116n38

Jungmann, J., 114n9

Justinian, 114n3

Kallistos, 7

Kierkegaard, Søren, xiii

Knowledge: apodictic, 8; dialectic, 8; God as "beyond knowledge," 13–15; of God, 6, 8–9, 12–15; human, 12–13; and unknowing, 13

Kokkinos, Philotheos, 7, 8, 12, 114n11, 115n13

Lex credendi, the, xii

Lex orandi, the, xii

Life: divine, 20; of Palamas, 5–10

Light: and darkness, 17; doctrine of "uncreated light,", xi; -experience, 17; hypostatic, 17; of Mt. Thabor (thaboric), xii, 7

Logos, the, 18, 19

Lossky, Vladimir, xiii

Luke, the Gospel of: 9:28–36, 17

Lyons, St. Irenaeus of, 18

Macarius the Great, St. (Pseudo Macarius), 3, 4, 15, 114n 9

Man: in Christ, 18; in communion with God, 18–19; created in image of God, 14, 18; deification of, 8; endowed with being and eternity, 18; the fallen state of, 15; in fellowship with God, 18; and the Holy Spirit, 18; sanctified in Baptism and Eucharist, 16; transcends his own nature, 14

Manicheism, 4

Marcel, Gabriel, xiii

Maritain, Jacques, xiii

Mark, the Gospel of, 9:2–9, 17

Matter: freedom from, 15; and the mind, 2–3; and the spirit, 15

Matthew, the Gospel of: 11:25, 12; 17:1–9, 17

Maximus the Confessor, St., 12, 13, 17, 18, 22, 116n23, 116n35

Messalian movement, the, 3–4, 5, 9, 20, 114n9

Messianic Age, the, 20

Meyendorff, John, ix, x, xiii

Michael VIII Palaeologus, 15

Middle Ages, the, 3–4

Mind, the: and knowledge of God, 6, 12, 14; and matter, 2–3; the nature of, 13; and prayer, 2–3; transfigured by grace, 12

Monasticism: cenobitic, 2; hesychast (anchorite, eremitic), 1–2; monastic spirituality, 20; and personal religious experience, 3; and the sacraments, 3; and social responsibility, 3. *See also* Hesychasm

Moses, 14, 21

INDEX

INDEX

Index to Text

160

INDEX

and Messalianism, 124n4; and
mysticism, 117n3; and natural
contemplation, 118n4, 120n31; and
negative theology, 118n5; the
orthodoxy of, 117n3; and Palamas,
117n1, 117n3, 118n4, 120n31, 121n6,
129n97; and personal experience of
God, 118n5; as a positivist, 117n3;
and prayer, 130n111; and secular
education, 117n3, 118n5; and visions,
59, 129n89, 132n16, 138n17;
mentioned, 127n59, 136n79, 141n73,
143n108, 144n117, 146n146, 150n42,
151n63, 151n64, 151n71, 152n94
Barlaamites, the, 118n6
Basil, St.: and *ascesis*, 83; and deification,
88, and energy, 95, 97, 131n6; and
essence, 95, 97, 131n6; and
experience, 87; and God as a unique
light, 74; and knowledge, 44; and
prescience of God, 96; and the Son
of God, 102, 103; and the Spirit of
God, 91, 101, 102; and the
Transfiguration, 76; and the
uncreated light, 80; mentioned,
151n71
Beautiful, the, 99
Beauty: of the Age to Come, 81; the
divine, 34; of God, 106; the light of
the essential *b.*, 80; the primordial,
33
Being, 99, 121n9
Benedict, St., 123n43
Body, the: of Christ, 76, 77, 88, 132n26,
134n53; contemplation and, 38; of
death, 41; deified, 57; as earthen
vessel, 42; and evil, 41; and fleshly
things, 50–51; and gifts of the Spirit,
52–53; is good, 124n5; glorified, 72,
131n7; as the house of God, 41; and
hypostatic light, 57; as instrument of
soul, 42–43; the Manichees and,
124n4; and the mind, 44, 47, 51; Paul
and, 50; pleasures (or passions) of,
51, 74; purified, 42, 103; and
recollection, 46–47; the resurrection
of, 129n91, 131n7; and the soul,
47–48, 51–53, 109–10, 125–26n36,

126n47, 126n48; and spirit, 51; as
temple of the Holy Spirit, 41; the
transformation of (or transfiguration
or deification of), 41–55, 57, 121n11,
126n36, 129n91, 136n82; mentioned:
119n26
Bogomils, the, 124n4
Breathing, controlled, 45–46, 126–27n50

Cain, 28
Cappadocian Fathers, the, 151n64
Cataphatic theology, 74, 121n9;
Chalcedon, Council of, 140n53
Christ Jesus. *See* Jesus Christ
Chrysostom, St. John, 73, 91, 96,
138n22
Church, the, 62, 91, 93, 98, 153n104
Climacus, St. John, 45, 125n34
Colossians: 1:12, 143n98; 2:8, 119n23; 2:9,
146n142; 2:18, 120n1; 2:19, 145n130;
3:11, 138n20
Commandments of God, the: and the
body, 55; and contemplation, 37,
61–62; and purification, 59, 103–04;
and true knowledge, 61–62, 67,
123n31
Communion with God, 33, 48
Compunction, 49, 128n76
Constantinople, 117n3
Contemplation: angelic, 151n74; and
ascesis, 128–29n85; as a divinisation,
34; of essence around God, 78; as a
free gift, 100; the goal of, 31; of the
glory of Christ, 60, 80; of the glory
of the divine nature, 60, 100; of God,
67, 68, 76, 100; of God's work in
creation, 120n35; ineffable, 38; and
knowledge, 31, 58–61, 133n34; and
light, 33, 57–61, 65–66, 102;
mystical, 38; natural, 118n4, 132n22,
133n29, 137n94; perfect, 36; the
power of, 150n56; pure, 72; purity
by, 134n49; of the Spirit, 76;
Stephen's, 104; the supernatural
power of, 37, 77; true, 60–61; as a
union; 34; of visions, 44; and vision
of the Infinite, 39. *See also*
Recollection, Reflection

161

INDEX

INDEX

INDEX

INDEX

INDEX

INDEX

INDEX

Negation: ascent by, 36; the excellence of God is beyond, 57, 121n9, 131n1; and union with God, 64–65, 110

Neo-Messalianism, 121n4

Neoplatonists, the, 117n3

Nēpsis, 124n11

Nicephorus Gregorus. See Gregorus, Nicephorus

Nineveh, St. Isaac of. See Isaac of Nineveh, St.

Noūs, the, 117–18n3; 124n11, 134n54, 135–36n69, 136n79

Numbers: 11:17, 145n136; 12:8, 138–39n22, 143n99, 143n105, 22:25, 132n15; 22:27, 132n15

Nyssa, St. Gregory of. See Gregory of Nyssa, St.

Obedience, 133n30

Obscurantism, 119n27

Old Law, the, 30–31

Omphalopsychoi, 127n59

Origen, 120n33, 123n32, 125n28, 125n31, 130n114

Orthodox, the, 64, 133n30

Paideia, 117n3

Palamas, Gregory of: and apophatic theology, 121n9; and Barlaam, 117n1, 117n3, 118n4, 120n30, 120n31, 129n97, 130n111, 132n17, 146n146, 147n5, 151n64, 153n113, 154n121, 154n131; and St. Benedict, 123n43; and the body, 129n105; and communion with God, 151n75; and contemplative tradition, 117n3, 133n34; and ecstasis, 129n106, 135n62; and the energies of God, 123n46; 142n79, 142n80, 142n81; and the essence of God, 123n46; 142n79, 142n80, 142n81; and Greek philosophy, 119n9, 126n48; and idolatry, 119n12; and levels of cognition, 135–36n69; and light, 150n48; and medicine, 120n30; and natural contemplation, 118n4, 137n94; and natural sciences, 130n113, 132n18; and polytheism, 119n10; and psychophysical method

of prayer, 126–27n50; and pure prayer, 122n25; and secular studies (or philosophy), 117n3, 119n27, 120n37; and the Spirit, 122n20; and the Sun, 134n52; and symbols, 139n34; theology of, 141n57; and vision of God, 121n11, 123n45, 132n17, 140n42, 141n67; mentioned, 121n6, 130n114, 133n39, 137n1, 142n81, 142n87

Panephysis, Joseph of, 131n7

Passion: and asceticism, 117n2, 128n75; evil, 49; the extirpation of, 122n25; liberation from, 49, 117n2; as the mark of error, 32; redirected, 130n114; rejecting, 49; the soul and, 51–52, 54–55; the tyranny of, 117n2, 128n75; victory over, 32; mentioned, 130n117

Patience, 46, 54

Paul the Apostle, St.: and the body, 50; and the gifts of the Spirit, 52–53; and human wisdom, 27, 29; heard ineffable words, 38; saw invisible things, 38; and light of revelation, 38, 57; was light and spirit, 66; as the mouthpiece of Christ, 30; participated in the life of the Spirit, 71; and the parts of the Spirit, 99; and predeterminations, 94; the rapture (or ecstasy) of, 66, 122n18, 129n106; became supracelestial, 34; mentioned, 28, 42, 47, 83, 88, 90, 106

Peace, 39, 90, 117n2

Pelagians, the, 122n23, 142n85

Pentecost, 91, 153n104

Perfection, 25, 86

1 Peter: 3:15, 118n7

2 Peter: 1:4, 152n97; 1:16, 133n40; 1:18, 133n44; 1:19, 133n45

Peter the Apostle, St., 62, 91, 133n40

Petrification, 49

Philosophy: the arrogance of, 29; as a gift of God, 27, 120n37; the legitimacy of, 119n27; "natural philosophy," 120n35; "outside philosophy," 120n40; Palamas and, 119n9, 126n48; does not save, 25–30; usefulness of, 28

INDEX

Plato, 117*n*3, 130*n*112, 134*n*52, 138*n*17
Platonism, 119*n*8, 125–26*n*36, 126*n*48, 141*n*74
Plotinus, 123*n*41
Polytheism, 26, 119*n*10
Positivism, 117*n*3
Power: divine, 109; of God, 59–60, 89, 93–94, 98, 99, 102–03; spiritual, 100; of vision, 101
Prayer: activism of, 122*n*23; and ascetical combat, 48–49; assiduity in, 39; Barlaam and, 130*n*111; and compunction, 49; and contemplation, 120*n*35; the end (goal) of, 64; and fasting, 49; hesychasts and, 32, 41–55; immaterial, 37, 58; inner, 48, 124*n*11, 126–27*n*50; and knowledge, 58–59; the mind and, 38, 42, 49, 50, 53, 54, 65, 127*n*51; as the mother of tears, 49; mysterious, 67; mystical, 67; and passions, 49; pure *p.*, 35, 37, 38, 49, 65, 122*n*25, 128*n*72, 130*n*115, 135*n*60; and purity of intellect, 38; and sensation, 128*n*72; union through, 37, 58, 64–65; the vision beyond, 35; mentioned, 47
Prescience, 93–94, 96, 147*n*5, 147*n*8
Principle: of deification, 87–88; the Divine, 39; the inner, 118*n*4; the more-than-, 39; of the universe, 99
Proverbs: 2:5, 123*n*32, 125*n*32; 12:13, 131*n*120; 13:9, 143*n*97; 27:21, 125*n*31
Providence, 59–60, 63, 74, 93, 94, 97, 147*n*3, 147*n*5, 147*n*8
Psalms: 7:10, 128*n*67; 32(33):6, 151*n*67; 35(36):10, 152*n*85; 36:9, 135*n*67; 44:14, 125*n*28; 46(47):10, 129*n*96; 51(50):19, 128*n*77; 102(103):18, 131*n*121; 103(104):2, 133*n*43; 138:12–13, 128*n*69
Pseudo-Denys. *See* Denys the Areopagite, Ps.
Purification, 58–59
Purity: blessed, 37, 84, 102, 109; purified body, 42, 103, 109; pure contemplation, 72; of heart, 35, 67–68, 122*n*25, 128*n*80, 140*n*42; and illumination, 102, 108; of the

intellect, 38; purest of lights, 89; pure love, 55; purified mind, 42, 55, 108–09, 154*n*119; purified of passions, 58, 132*n*17; pure prayer, 35, 37, 38, 49, 65, 67, 122*n*25, 130*n*115; purified soul, 88, 103, 109, 132*n*161; sublime, 90; mentioned, 130*n*117

Quiet, Inner, 46, 67, 127*n*54, 135*n*62, 137*n*88

Radiance of God, the, 33, 83, 110
Reality, the Divine, 64, 81, 82, 121*n*9
Reason, 43, 52, 54, 66, 119*n*10, 119*n*27, 120*n*35, 120*n*37, 130*n*112
Recollection, 44–46, 48, 125*n*25, 126*n*44, 126*n*47, 130*n*115. *See also* Contemplation, Reflection
Redemption, 91
Reflection, 46, 48. *See also* Contemplation, Recollection
Regeneration, 47
Remembrance of God, 54, 130*n*111
Resurrection, the: the final, 136*n*82; of the righteous, 72; the sons of, 67; mentioned, 134*n*50
Revelation, 38
Revelation, the Book of: 1:23, 128*n*67; 21:23–24, 138*n*14; 22:5, 138*n*14
Romans: 1:22, 119*n*19; 5:6, 152*n*83; 6:23, 128*n*61; 7:2, 124*n*10; 7:14, 124*n*7; 7:18, 124*n*8; 7:23, 124*n*9; 7:24, 124*n*7; 8:23, 136*n*82; 12:1, 131*n*119

Salvation, 25–30
Sanctification, 91, 138*n*11, 142*n*85
Sciences, the natural, 119*n*27
Scripture: the authority of, 117*n*3; light from, 63; the teaching of, 59; truth of, 144*n*49; visions and, 59; mentioned, 32, 33, 47, 48, 55, 78, 121*n*13
Second Coming, the, 138*n*15
Sensation: and fasting, 48; intellectual, 37; and prayer, 128*n*72; spiritual, 37
Senses, the: and the Age to Come, 108; and the knowledge of God, 69; and the mind, 118–19*n*8; and nonbeing

INDEX

Tongues, the gift of, 52–53

Transcendence: of God, 71, 84, 87, 95–98, 110, 122n22; nonbeing by, 66; self-, 122n24, 145n126

Transfiguration: the Feast of, 74, 139n28, 140n44, 140n45; illumination at the, 31, 63, 72, 138n13, 139–40n38; of saints, 131n7; of the spiritual intellect, 121n13; of the whole person, 121n11, 136n82; mentioned, 136n84, 138–39n22, 140n41

Trinity, the Holy: the glory of, 33, 77, 139n28; the light of, 38, 129n89; the nature of, 97; the uncreated, 97

Truth: acquisition of, 28; defending, 145n125; the firmness of, 32; pagan philosophy and, 120n29; the simplicity of, 32; the Spirit of God instructs man in, 103

Union: with better things, 58; the divine, 50, 83; with God, 50, 52–55, 64–65, 84, 87, 109–10, 134n55, 135n67, 136n70, 142n88, 143n107, 144n117, 145n127; hypostatic, 88; with illumination, 100; and intellectual sensation, 37; the light of, 91; with light, 38, 65–66; with mystery of divine simplicity, 109; mystical, 135n64, 135n65, 135–36n69; unified recollection, 46

Universe, the Principle of, 99

Unknowing, 32, 36, 117n3, 121n9

Via negativa, the, 118n5, 123n30

Virgin, the, 89

Virtue: to acquire, 43–44; and deification, 83; and impassibility, 54; the prize of, 89; stability in, 117n2; the struggle for, 44; as unoriginate, 94–95; and vision of God, 146n154

Vision: of angels, 58; Barlaam and, 59, 129n89, 132n16, 138n17; the eternal, 100; of God, 32–33, 38–39, 58–59, 67, 121n9, 121n11, 122n19, 122n23, 123n30, 123n44, 123n45, 128–29n85, 129n91, 132n16, 132n22, 135n63, 135n65, 135n67, 138n13, 140n42, 141n63, 141n67, 146n154, 150n44, 154n131; and ignorance, 58–59; of the Infinite, 39; intelligible, 44; and light, 59, 62–63, 65, 135n66; the light of, 101; the man of, 84; mystical, 38, 58, 117n3; the Object of, 39; the power of, 101; Stephen's, 152n88; true, 58–59; and the uncreated light of the Trinity, 129n89

Will, the Divine, 55, 82, 94, 105, 106

Wisdom: of this age, 27; from experience, 59; foolish, 26, 27; as gift of God, 30; of God, 26, 28, 59–60, 91; Greek, 27; human, 26–27; the knowledge beyond, 36; and knowledge of the natural world, 118n6; profane, 29; sacred, 30; of the saints, 59; secular, 25–26, 29; and study, 83; mentioned, 98

Wisdom, the Book of: 1:7, 146n144

Word, the: Christ as, 34, 94; of Christ, 61; the divinity of, 33; dwelling in man, 106; of God, 51, 94, 107; the grace of, 33

Word of instruction, the gift of, 52–53

Works of God, the, 51, 94–95, 97, 106, 147n15

World Soul, the, 26

Yoga, 127n59

Zachariah, 75, 139n35

172

Other Volumes in this Series

Sharafuddin Maneri • THE HUNDRED LETTERS

Martin Luther • THEOLOGIA GERMANICA

Native Mesoamerican Spirituality • ANCIENT MYTHS, DISCOURSES, STORIES, DOCTRINES, HYMNS, POEMS FROM THE AZTEC, YUCATEC, QUICHE-MAYA AND OTHER SACRED TRADITIONS

Symeon the New Theologian • THE DISCOURSES

Ibn Al'-Arabī • THE BEZELS OF WISDOM

Hadewijch • THE COMPLETE WORKS

Philo of Alexandria • THE CONTEMPLATIVE LIFE, THE GIANTS, AND SELECTIONS

George Herbert • THE COUNTRY PARSON, THE TEMPLE

Unknown • THE CLOUD OF UNKNOWING

John and Charles Wesley • SELECTED WRITINGS AND HYMNS

Meister Eckhart • THE ESSENTIAL SERMONS, COMMENTARIES, TREATISES AND DEFENSE

Francisco de Osuna • THE THIRD SPIRITUAL ALPHABET

Jacopone da Todi • THE LAUDS

Fakhruddin 'Iraqi • DIVINE FLASHES

Menahem Nahum of Chernobyl • THE LIGHT OF THE EYES

Early Dominicans • SELECTED WRITINGS

John Climacus • THE LADDER OF DIVINE ASCENT

Francis and Clare • THE COMPLETE WORKS